Penguin Books
Foreign Affairs and other stories

Sean O'Faolain was born in 1900 and educated at the National
University of Ireland. For a year he was a commercial
traveller for books but gave it up to fight on the side of
de Valera in 1921. He was a member of the Irish Republican
Army for six years, taught for a further year and then studied
for three years at Harvard University. For four years he
taught at Strawberry Hill Training College for Teachers, after
which he turned to writing and went back to his native
Ireland, where he now lives in Dublin. He has written some
twenty books, including *The Irish* (a Pelican book) and travel
and literary criticism, novels, biographies, and several books
of short stories. He has also contributed to all the well-known
periodicals in Great Britain and the United States. His more
recent publications are an autobiography, *Vive Moi!*, a book of
stories, *The Heat of the Sun*, *The Talking Trees* and *Foreign
Affairs*. Sean O'Faolain is a D.Litt. of Trinity College, Dublin.
He is married, with two children. His wife has written several
books of Irish folk-tales and his daughter published her first
book of stories in 1968.

Sean O'Faolain

Foreign Affairs
and other stories

Penguin Books

Penguin Books Ltd, Harmondsworth,
Middlesex, England
Penguin Books, 625 Madison Avenue,
New York, New York 10022, U.S.A.
Penguin Books Australia Ltd, Ringwood,
Victoria, Australia
Penguin Books Canada Ltd, 2801 John Street,
Markham, Ontario, Canada L3R 1B4
Penguin Books (N.Z.) Ltd, 182–190 Wairau Road,
Auckland 10, New Zealand

First published in Great Britain by
Constable and Company Ltd 1976
Published in Penguin Books 1978

Copyright © Sean O'Faolain, 1971, 1973, 1974, 1975, 1976
All rights reserved

Five of these stories have appeared in *Playboy*,
in which *Something, Everything, Anything, Nothing*
was entitled *Venus or the Virgin*. One of the
stories has appeared in *Winter's Tales* (Macmillan)
and one in *The Atlantic Monthly*

Made and printed in Great Britain by
Cox & Wyman Ltd., London, Reading and Fakenham
Set in Intertype Times

Except in the United States of America, this book is
sold subject to the condition that it shall not, by
way of trade or otherwise, be lent, re-sold, hired out,
or otherwise circulated without the publisher's prior
consent in any form of binding or cover other than
that in which it is published and without a similar
condition including this condition being imposed on
the subsequent purchaser

For Robie Macauley

Contents

The Faithless Wife

He had now been stalking his beautiful Mlle Morphy, whose
real name was Mrs Meehawl O'Sullivan, for some six weeks,
and she had appeared to be so amused at every stage of the
hunt, so responsive, *entrainante*, even *aguichante*, that he could
already foresee the kill over the next horizon. At their first
encounter, during the Saint Patrick's Day cocktail party at the
Dutch embassy, accompanied by a husband who had not a
word to throw to a cat about anything except the scissors and
shears that he manufactured somewhere in the West of Ireland,
and who was obviously quite ill at ease and drank too much
Irish whiskey, what had attracted him to her was not only her
splendid Boucher figure (whence his sudden nickname for her,
La Morphée), or her copper-coloured hair, her lime-green Irish
eyes and her seemingly poreless skin, but her calm, total and
subdued elegance: the Balenciaga costume, the peacock-skin
gloves, the gleaming crocodile handbag, a glimpse of tiny, lace-
edged lawn handkerchief and her dry, delicate scent. He had a
grateful eye and nose for such things. It was, after all, part of his
job. Their second meeting, two weeks later, at his own embassy,
had opened the doors. She came alone.

Now, at last, inside a week, perhaps less, there would be an
end to all the probationary encounters that followed – mostly
her inventions, at his persistent appeals – those wide-eyed fancy-
meeting-you-heres at the zoo, at race-meetings, afternoon
cinemas, in art galleries, at more diplomatic parties (once he
had said gaily to her, 'The whole diplomacy of Europe seems to
circle around our interest in one another'), those long drives
over the Dublin mountains in his Renault coupé, those titillating
rural lunches, nose to nose, toe to toe (rural because she quickly
educated him to see Dublin as a stock exchange for gossip, a

9

casino of scandal), an end, which was rather a pity, to those charming unforeseen-foreseen, that is to say proposed but in the end just snatched, afternoon *promenades champêtres* under the budding leaves and closing skies of the Phoenix Park, with the first lights of the city springing up below them to mark the end of another boring day for him in Ailesbury Road, Dublin's street of embassies, for her another possibly cosier but, he selfishly hoped, not much more exciting day in her swank boutique on Saint Stephen's Green. Little by little those intimate encounters, those murmured confessions had lifted acquaintance to friendship, to self-mocking smiles over some tiny incident during their last meeting, to eager anticipation of the next, an aimless tenderness twanging to appetite like an arrow. Or, at least, that was how he felt about it all. Any day now, even any hour, the slow countdown, slower than the slow movement of Mendelssohn's Concerto in E Minor, or the most swoony sequence from the Siegfried Idyll, or that floating spun-sugar balloon of Mahler's 'Song of the Earth,' to the music of which on his gramophone he would imagine her smiling sidelong at him as she softly disrobed, and his ingenious playing with her, his teasing and warming of her moment by moment for the roaring, blazing takeoff. To the moon!

Only one apprehension remained with him, not a real misgiving, something nearer to a recurring anxiety. It was that at the last moments when her mind and her body ought to take leave of one another she might take to her heels. It was a fear that flooded him whenever, with smiles too diffident to reassure him, she would once again mention that she was a Roman Catholic, or a Cat, a Papist or a Pape, a convent girl, and once she laughed that during her schooldays in the convent she had actually been made an *Enfant de Marie*. The words never ceased to startle him, dragging him back miserably to his first sexual frustration with his very pretty but unexpectedly proper cousin Berthe Ohnet during his lycée years in Nancy; a similar icy snub a few years later in Quebec; repeated still later by that smack on the face in Rio that almost became a public scandal; memories so painful that whenever an attractive woman nowadays mentioned religion, even in so simple a context as, 'Thank God

I didn't buy that hat, or frock, or stock, or mare,' a red flag at once began to flutter in his belly.

Obsessed, every time she uttered one of those ominous words he rushed for the reassurance of what he called The Sherbet Test, which meant observing the effect on her of some tentatively sexy joke, like the remark of the young princess on tasting her first sherbet: 'Oh, how absolutely delicious! But what a pity it isn't a sin!' To his relief she not only always laughed merrily at his stories but always capped them, indeed at times so startling him by her coarseness that it only occurred to him quite late in their day that this might be her way of showing her distaste for his diaphanous indelicacies. He had once or twice observed that priests, peasants and children will roar with laughter at some scavenger joke, and growl at even a veiled reference to a thigh. Was she a child of nature? Still, again and again back would come those disturbing words. He could have understood them from a prude, but what on earth did *she* mean by them? Were they so many herbs to season her desire with pleasure in her naughtiness? Flicks of nasty puritan sensuality to whip her body over some last ditch of indecision? It was only when the final crisis came that he wondered if this might not all along have been her way of warning him that she was neither a light nor a lecherous woman, neither a flirt nor a flibbertigibbet, that in matters of the heart she was *une femme très sérieuse*.

He might have guessed at something like it much earlier. He knew almost from the first day that she was *bien élevée*, her father a judge of the Supreme Court, her uncle a monsignor at the Vatican, a worldly, sport-loving, learned, contriving priest who had persuaded her papa to send her for a finishing year to Rome with the Sisters of the Sacred Heart at the top of the Spanish Steps; chiefly, it later transpired, because the convent was near the *centre hippique* in the Borghese Gardens and it was his right reverend's opinion that no Irish girl could possibly be said to have completed her education until she had learned enough about horses to ride to hounds. She had told him a lot, and most amusingly, about this uncle. She had duly returned from Rome to Dublin, and whenever he came over for the hunting, he always rode beside her. This attention had mightily

11

flattered her until she discovered that she was being used as a cover for his uncontrollable passion for Lady Kinvara and Loughrea, then the master, some said the mistress, of the Clare-Galway hounds.

'How old were you then?' Ferdy asked, fascinated.

'I was at the university. Four blissful, idling years. But I got my degree. I was quick. And,' she smiled, 'good-looking. It helps, even with professors.'

'But riding to hounds as a student?'

'Why not? In Ireland everybody does. Children do. You could ride to hounds on a plough horse if you had nothing else. So long as you keep out of the way of real hunters. I only stopped after my marriage, when I had a miscarriage. And I swear that was only because I was thrown.'

A monsignor who was sport-loving, worldly and contriving. He understood, and approved, and it explained many things about her.

The only other ways in which her dash, beauty and gaiety puzzled and beguiled him were trivial. Timid she was not, she was game for any risk. But the coolness of her weather eye often surprised him.

'The Leopardstown Races? Oh, what a good idea, Ferdy! Let's meet there ... The Phoenix Park Races? No, not there. Too many doctors showing off their wives and their cars, trying to be noticed. And taking notice. Remember, a lot of my college friends married doctors ... No, not *that* cinema. It has become vogueish ... In fact, no cinema on the south side of the river. What we want is a good old fleabitten picture house on the north side where they show nothing but westerns and horrors, and where the kids get in on Saturday mornings for thruppence ... Oh, and do please only ring the boutique in an emergency. Girls gossip.'

Could she be calculating? For a second of jealous heat he wondered if she could possibly have another lover. Cooling, he saw that if he had to keep a wary eye in his master's direction she had to think of her bourgeois clientele. Besides, he was a bachelor, and would remain one. She had to manage her inexpressibly dull, if highly successful, old scissors and shears manufacturer, well past fifty and probably as suspicious as he was boring; so intensely, so exhaustingly boring that the only subject about which she could herself nearly become boring was in her frequent complaints about his boringness. Once she *was* frightening – when she spat out that she had hated her husband ever since the first night of their marriage when he brought her for their honeymoon – it was odd how long, and how intensely this memory had rankled – not, as he had promised, to Paris, but to his bloody scissors and shears factory in the wet wilds of northern Donegal. ('Just me dear, haha, to let 'em see, haha, t'other half of me scissors.')

Ferdy had of course never asked her why she had married such a cretin; not after sizing up her house, her furniture, her pictures, her clothes, her boutique. Anyway, only another cretin would discourage any pretty woman from grumbling about her husband: (*a*) because such grumblings give a man a chance to show what a deeply sympathetic nature he has, and (*b*) because the information incidentally supplied helps one to arrange one's assignations in places and at times suitable to all concerned.

Adding it all up (he was a persistent adder-upper) only one problem had so far defeated him: that he was a foreigner and did not know what sort of women Irish women are. It was not as if he had not done his systematic best to find out, beginning with a course of reading through the novels of her country. A vain exercise. With the exception of the Molly Bloom of James Joyce the Irish Novel had not only failed to present him with any fascinating women but had presented him with, in his sense of the word, no woman at all. Irish fiction was a lot of nineteenth-century *connerie* about half-savage Brueghelesque peasants, or urban *petits fonctionnaires* who invariably solved their frustrations by getting drunk on religion, patriotism or undiluted whiskey, or by taking flight to England. Pastoral melodrama. (Giono at his worst.) Or pastoral humbuggery. (Bazin at his most sentimental.) Or, at its best, pastoral lyricism. (Daudet and rosewater.) As for Molly Bloom! He enjoyed the smell of every kissable pore of her voluptuous body without for one moment believing that she had ever existed. James Joyce in drag.

'But,' he had finally implored his best friend in Ailesbury Road, Hamid Bey, the third secretary of the Turkish embassy, whose amorous secrets he willingly purchased with his own, 'if it is too much to expect Ireland to produce a bevy of Manons, Mitsous, Gigis, Claudines, Kareninas, Oteros, Leahs, San Severinas, what about those great-thighed, vast-bottomed creatures dashing around the country on horseback like Diana followed by all her minions? Are they not interested in love? And if so why aren't there novels about them?'

His friend laughed as toughly as Turkish Delight and replied in English in his laziest Noel Coward drawl, all the vowels frontal as if he were talking through bubble gum, all his r's either left out where they should be, as in *deah* or *cleah*, or inserted where they should not be, as in *India-r* or *Iowa-r*.

'My deah Ferdy, did not your deah fatheh or your deah mamma-r eveh tell you that all Irish hohsewomen are in love with their hohses? And anyway it is well known that the favourite pin-up gihl of Ahĺand is a gelding.'

'Naked?' Ferdinand asked coldly, and refused to believe him, remembering that his beloved had been a hohsewoman, and satisfied that he was not a gelding. Instead, he approached the Italian ambassador at a cocktail party given by the Indonesian embassy to whisper to him about *l'amore irlandese* in his best stage French, and stage French manner, eyebrows lifted above fluttering eyelids, voice as hoarse as, he guessed, His Excellency's mind would be on its creaking way back to memories of Gabin, Jouvet, Brasseur, Fernandel, Yves Montand. It proved to be another futile exercise. His Ex groaned as operatically as every Italian groans over such vital, and lethal, matters as the Mafia, food, taxation and women, threw up his hands, made a face like a more than usually desiccated De Sica and sighed, 'Les femmes d'Irlande? Mon pauvre gars! Elles sont d'une chasteté . . .' He paused and roared the adjective, '. . . FOR-MIDABLE!'

Ferdinand had heard this yarn about feminine chastity in other countries and (with those two or three exceptions already mentioned), found it true only until one had established the precise local variation of the meaning of 'chastity.' But how was he to discover the Irish variation? In the end it was Celia herself who, unwittingly, revealed it to him and in doing so dispelled his last doubts about her susceptibility, inflammability and volatility – despite the very proper Sisters of the Spanish Steps.

The revelation occurred one night in early May – her Meehawl being away in the West, presumably checking what she contemptuously called his Gaelic-squeaking scissors. Ferdy had driven her back to his flat for a nightcap after witnessing the prolonged death of Mimi in *La Bohème*. She happened to quote to him Oscar Wilde's remark about the death of Little Nell that only a man with a heart of stone could fail to laugh at it, and in this clever vein they had continued for a while over the rolling brandy, seated side by side on his settee, his hand on her bare shoulder leading him to hope more and more fondly that this might be his Horizon Night, until, suddenly, she asked him a coldly probing question.

'Ferdy! Tell me exactly why we did not believe in the reality of Mimi's death.'

His palm oscillated gently between her clavicle and her scapula.

'Because, my little cabbage, we were not expected to. Singing away like a lark? With her last breath? And no lungs? I am a Frenchman. I understand the nature of reality and can instruct you about it. Art, my dear Celia, is art because it is not reality. It does not copy or represent nature. It improves upon it. It embellishes it. This is the kernel of the classical French attitude to life. And,' he beamed at her, 'to love. We make of our wildest feelings of passion the gentle art of love.'

He suddenly stopped fondling her shoulder and surveyed her with feelings of chagrin and admiration. The sight of her belied his words. Apart from dressing with taste, and, he felt certain, undressing with even greater taste, she used no art at all. She was an innocent of makeup as a peasant girl of the Vosges. Had he completely misread her? Was she that miracle, a fully ripe peach brought into the centre of the city some twenty years ago from a walled garden in the heart of the country, still warm from the sun, still glowing, downy, pristine, innocent as the dew? He felt her juice dribbling down the corner of his mouth.

15

Was this the missing piece of her jigsaw? An ensealed innocence. If so he had wasted six whole weeks. This siege could last six years.

'No, Ferdy!' she said crossly. 'You have it all wrong. I'm talking about life, not about art. The first and last thought of any real Italian girl on her deathbed would be to ask for a priest. She was facing her God.'

God at once pointed a finger at him through the chandelier, and within seconds they were discussing love among the English, Irish, French, Indians, Moslems, Italians, naturally the Papacy, Alexander the Sixth and incest, Savonarola and dirty pictures, Joan of Arc and martyrdom, death, sin, hellfire, Cesare Borgia who, she insisted, screamed for a priest to pray for him at the end.

'A lie,' he snarled, 'that some beastly priest told you in a sermon when you were a schoolgirl. Pray! I suppose,' he challenged furiously, 'you pray even against me.'

Abashed, she shook her autumn-brown head at him, threw a kipper-eyed glance up to the chandelier, gave him a ravishingly penitential smile, and sighed like an unmasked sinner.

'Ah, Ferdy! Ferdy! If you only knew the real truth about me! Me pray against you? I don't pray at all. You remember Mimi's song at the end of the first act? "I do not always go to Mass, but I pray quite a bit to the good Lord." Now, I hedge my bets in a very different way. I will not pray because I refuse to go on my knees to anybody. Yet, there I go meekly trotting off to Mass every Sunday and holy day. And why? Because I am afraid not to, because it would be a mortal sin not to.' She gripped his tensed hand, trilling her r's over the threshold of her lower lip and tenderly umlauting her vowels. Dürling. Cöward. Li-er. 'Amn't I the weak cöward, dürling? Amn't I the awful li-er? A crook entirrrely?'

Only a thin glint of streetlight peeping between his curtains witnessed the wild embrace of a man illuminated by an avowal so patently bogus as to be the transparent truth.

'You a liar?' he gasped, choking with laughter. 'You a shivering coward? A double-faced hedger of bets? A deceiving crook? A wicked sinner? For the last five minutes you have been every single one of them by pretending to be them. What you really are is a woman full of cool, hard-headed discretion, which you would like to sell to me as a charming weakness. Full of dreams that you would like to disguise as wicked lies. Of common sense that it suits you to pass off as crookedness. Of worldly wisdom still moist from your mother's nipple that, if you thought you would get away with the deception, you would stoop to call a sin. My dearest Celia, your yashmak reveals by pretending to conceal. Your trick is to be innocence masquerading as villainy. I think it is enchanting.'

For the first time he saw her in a rage.

'But it is *all* true. I *am* a liar. I *do* go to Mass every Sunday. I do *not* pray. I *am* afraid of damnation. I . . .'

He silenced her with three fingers laid momentarily on her lips.

'Of course you go to Mass every Sunday. My father, a master tailor of Nancy, used to go to Mass every Sunday not once but three times, and always as conspicuously as possible. Why? Because he was a tailor, just as you run a boutique. You don't pray? Sensible woman. Why should you bother your *bon Dieu*, if there is a *bon Dieu*, with your pretty prattle about things that He knew all about one billion years before you were a wink in your mother's eye? My dearest and perfect love, you have told me everything about Irishwomen that I need to know. None of you says what you think. Every one of you means what you don't say. None of you thinks about what she is going to do. But every one of you knows it to the last dot. You dream like opium eaters and your eyes are as calm as resting snow. You are all of you realists to your bare backsides. Yes, yes, yes, yes, yes, you will say this is true of all women, but it is not. It is not even true of Frenchwomen. They may be realists in lots of things. In love, they are just as stupid as all the rest of us. But not Irishwomen! Or not, I swear it, if they are all like you. I'll prove it to you with a single question. Would you, like Mimi, live for the sake of love in a Paris garret?'

She gravely considered a proposition that sounded delightfully like a proposal.

'How warm would the garret be? Would I have to die of tuberculosis? You remember how the poor Bohemian dramatist had to burn his play to keep them all from being famished with the cold.'

'Yes!' Ferdy laughed. 'And as the fire died away he said, "I always knew that last act was too damned short." But you are dodging my question.'

'I suppose, dürling, any woman's answer to your question would depend on how much she was in love with whoever he was. Or wouldn't it?'

Between delight and fury he dragged her into his arms.

'You know perfectly well, you sweet slut, that what I am asking you is, "Do you love me a lot or a little? A garretful or a palaceful?" which is it?'

Chuckling she slid down low in the settee and smiled up at him between sleepycat eyelashes.

'And you, Ferdy, must know perfectly well that it is pointless to ask any woman silly questions like that. If some man I loved very much were to ask me, "Do you love me, Celia?" I would naturally answer, "No!", in order to make him love me more. And if it was some man I did not like at all I would naturally say, "Yes, I love you so much I think we ought to get married," in order to cool him off. Which, Ferdy, do you want me to say to you?'

'Say,' he whispered adoringly, 'that you hate me beyond the tenth circle of Dante's hell.'

She made a grave face.

'I'm afraid, Ferdy, the fact is I don't like you at all. Not at all! Not one least little bit at all, at all.'

At which lying, laughing, enlacing and unlacing moment they kissed pneumatically and he knew that if all Irishwomen were Celias then the rest of mankind were mad ever to have admired women of any other race.

Their lovemaking was not as he had foredreamed it. She hurled her clothes to the four corners of the room, crying out, 'And about time too! Ferdy, what the hell have you been fooling around for during the last six weeks?' Within five minutes she smashed him into bits. In her passion she was more like a lion than a lioness. There was nothing about her either titillating or erotic, indolent or indulgent, as wild, as animal, as unrestrained, as simple as a forest fire. When, panting beside her, he recovered enough breath to speak he expressed his surprise that one so cool, so ladylike in public could be so different in private. She grunted peacefully and said in her muted brogue, 'Ah, shure, dürling, everything changes in the beddaroom.'

He woke at three twenty-five in the morning with that clear bang so familiar to everybody who drinks too much after the chimes of midnight, rose to drink a pint of cold water, lightly opened his curtains to survey the pre-dawn May sky and, turning towards the bed, saw the pallid streetlamp's light fall across her sleeping face, as calm, as soothed, as innocently sated as a baby filled with its mother's milk. He sat on the side of the bed looking down at her for a long time, overcome by the terrifying knowledge that, for the first time in his life, he had fallen in love.

The eastern clouds were growing as pink as petals while they drank the coffee he had quietly prepared. Over it he arranged in unnecessarily gasping whispers for their next meeting the following afternoon – '*This* afternoon!' he said joyously – at three twenty-five, henceforth his Mystic Hour for Love, but only on the strict proviso that he would not count on her unless she had set three red geraniums in a row on the windowsill of her boutique before three o'clock and that she, for her part, must divine a tragedy if the curtains of his flat were not looped high when she approached at three twenty o'clock. He could, she knew, have more easily checked with her by telephone, but also knowing how romantically, voluptuously, erotically minded he was she accepted with an indulgent amusement what he obviously considered ingenious devices for increasing the voltage of passion by the trappings of conspiracy. To herself she thought, 'Poor boy! He's been reading too many dirty books.'

Between two o'clock and three o'clock that afternoon she was entertained to see him pass her boutique three times in dark glasses. She cruelly made him pass a fourth time before, precisely at three o'clock, she gave him the pleasure of seeing two white hands with pink fingernails – not, wickedly, her own: her assistant's – emerge from under the net curtains of her window to arrange three small scarlet geraniums on the sill. He must have hastened perfervidly to the nearest florist to purchase the pink roses whose petals – when she rang his bell five cruel moments after his Mystic Hour – she found (to her tolerant amusement at his boyish folly) tessellating the silk sheets of his bed. His gramophone, muted by a bath towel, was murmuring Wagner. A joss stick in a brass bowl stank cloyingly. He had cast a pink silk headscarf over the bedside lamp. His dressing-table mirror had been tilted so that from where they lay they could see themselves. Within five minutes he neither saw, heard nor smelled anything, tumbling, falling, hurling headlong to consciousness of her mocking laughter at the image of her bottom mottled all over by his clinging rose petals. It cost him a brutal effort to laugh at himself.

All that afternoon he talked only of flight, divorce and re-marriage. To cool him she encouraged him. He talked of it again and again every time they met. Loving him she humoured him. On the Wednesday of their third week as lovers they met briefly and chastely because her Meehawl was throwing a dinner at his house that evening for a few of his business colleagues previous to flying out to Manchester for a two-day convention of cutlers. Ferdy at once promised her to lay in a store of champagne, caviar, *pâté de foie* and brioches so that they need not stir from their bed for the whole of those two days.

'Not even once?' she asked coarsely, and he made a moue of disapproval.

'You do not need to be all that realistic, Celia!'

Already by three fifteen that Thursday afternoon he was shuffling nervously from window to window. By three twenty-five he was muttering, 'I hope she's not going to be late.' He kept feeling the champagne to be sure it was not getting too cold. At three thirty-five he moaned, 'She *is* late!' At three forty he cried out in a jealous fury, glaring up and down the street, 'The slut is betraying me!' At a quarter to four his bell rang, he leaped to the door. She faced him as coldly as a newly carved statue of Carrara marble. She repulsed his arms. She would not stir beyond his doormat. Her eyes were dilated by fear.

'It is Meehawl!' she whispered.

'He has found us out?'

'It's the judgement of God on us both!'

The word smacked his face.

'He is dead?' he cried hopefully, brushing aside fear and despair.

'A stroke.'

She made a violent, downward swish with the side of her open palm.

'Une attaque? De paralysie?'

'He called at the boutique on his way to the plane. He said goodbye to me. He walked out to the taxi. I went into my office to prepare my vanity case and do peepee before I met you. The taxi driver ran in shouting that he had fallen in a fit on the pavement. We drove him to 96. That's Saint Vincent's. The hospital near the corner of the Green. He is conscious. But he cannot speak. One side of him is paralysed. He may not live. He has had a massive coronary.'

She turned and went galloping down the stairs.

His immediate rebound was to roar curses on all the gods that never were. Why couldn't the old fool have his attack next week? His second thought was glorious. 'He will die, we will get married.' His third made him weep, 'Poor little cabbage!' His fourth thought was, 'The brioches I throw out, the rest into the fridge.' His fifth, sixth and seventh were three Scotches while he rationally considered all her possible reactions to the brush of the dark angel's wing. Only Time, he decided, would tell.

But when liars become the slaves of Time what can Time do but lie like them? A vat solid-looking enough for old wine, it leaks at every stave. A ship rigged for the wildest seas, it is rustbound to its bollards on the quay. She said firmly that nothing between them could change. He refuted her. Everything had changed, and for the better. He rejoiced when the doctors said their patient was doomed. After two more weeks she reported that the doctors were impressed by her husband's remarkable tenacity. He spoke of Flight. She now spoke of Time. One night as she lay hot in his arms in his bed he shouted triumphantly to the chandelier that when husbands are imprisoned lovers are free. She demurred. She could never spend a

21

night with him in her own bed; not with a resident housekeeper upstairs. He tossed it aside. What matter where they slept! He would be happy sleeping with her in the Phoenix Park. She pointed out snappishly that it was raining. 'Am I a seal?' He proffered her champagne. She confessed the awful truth. This night was the last night they could be together anywhere.

'While he was dying, a few of his business pals used to call on him at the Nursing Home – the place all Dublin knows as 96. Now that the old devil is refusing to die they refuse to call on him anymore. I am his only faithful visitor. He so bores everybody. And with his paralysed mouth they don't know what the hell he is saying. Do you realize, Ferdy, what this means? He is riding me like a nightmare. Soaking me up like blotting paper. He rang me four times the day before yesterday at the boutique. He rang again while I was here with you having a drink. He said whenever I go out I must leave a number where he can call me. The night before last he rang me at three o'clock in the morning. Thank God I was back in my own bed and not here with you. He said he was lonely. Has terrible dreams. That the nights are long. That he is frightened. That if he gets another stroke he will die. Dürling! I can never spend a whole night with you again!'

Ferdy became Napoleon. He took command of the campaign. He accompanied her on her next visit to 96. This, he discovered, was a luxury (i.e., Victorian) nursing home in Lower Leeson Street, where cardinals died, coal fires were in order, and everybody was presented with a menu from which to choose his lunch and dinner. The carpets were an inch thick. The noisiest internal sound heard was the Mass bell tinkling along the corridors early every morning as the priest went from room to room with the Eucharist for the dying faithful. The Irish, he decided, know how to die. Knowing no better, he bore with him copies of *Le Canard Enchainé, La Vie Parisienne*, and *Playboy*. Celia deftly impounded them. 'Do you want him to die of blood pressure? Do you want the nuns to think he's an Irish queer? A fellow who prefers women to drink?' Seated at one side of the bed, facing her seated at the other, he watched her, with her delicate lace-edged handkerchief (so disturbingly

reminiscent of her lace-edged panties) wiping the unshaven chin
of the dribbling half-idiot on the pillow. In an unconsumed rage
he lifted his eyebrows into his hair, surveyed the moving mass
of clouds above Georgian Dublin, smoothened his already
blackboard-smooth hair, gently touched the white carnation in
his lapel, forced himself to listen calmly to the all-but-unintel-
ligible sounds creeping from the dribbling corner of the twisted
mouth in the unshaven face of the revolting cretin on the
pillow beneath his eyes, and agonizingly asked himself by
what unimaginably devious machinery, and for what indi-
vinable purpose the universe had been so arranged since the
beginning of Time that this bronze-capped, pastel-eyed, rosy-
breasted, round-buttocked, exquisite flower of paradise sitting
opposite to him should, in the first place, have matched and
mated with this slob between them, and then, or rather *and
then*, or rather AND THEN make it so happen that he, Ferdinand Louis Jean-Honoré Clichy, of 9 *bis* rue des Domi-
nicains, Nancy, in the Department of Moselle et Meurthe,
population 133,532, altitude 212 metres, should happen to discover her in remote Dublin, and fall so utterly into her power
that if he were required at that particular second to choose
between becoming Ambassador to the Court of Saint James's
for life and one night alone in bed with her he would have at
once replied, 'Even for one hour!'

He gathered that the object on the pillow was addressing him.

'Oh, Mosheer! Thacks be to the ever cliving and cloving Gog
I khav mosht devote clittle wife in all Khlistendom ... I'd be
chlost without her ... Ah, Mosheer! If you ever dehide to
marry, marry an Irikhwoman ... Mosht fafeful cleatures in all
exhishtench ... Would any Frenchwoman attend shoopid ole
man chlike me the way Chelia doesh?'

Ferdy closed his eyes. She was tenderly dabbing the spittled
corners of the distorted mouth. What happened next was that a
Sister took Celia out to the corridor for a few private words and
that Ferdy at once leaned forward and whispered savagely to
the apparently immortal O'Sullivan, 'Monsieur O'Sullivan, your
wife does not look at all well. I fear she is wilting under the
strain of your illness.'

'Chlstrain!' the idiot said in astonishment. 'What chlstrain? I khlsee no khlsignch of kkchlstrain!'

Ferdy whispered with fierceness that when one is gravely ill one may sometimes fail to observe the grave illness of others.

'We have to remember, Monsieur, that if your clittle wife were to collapse under the chlstr . . . under the *strain* of your illness it would be very serious, for *you*!'

After that day the only reason he submitted to accompany his love on these painful and piteous visits to 96 was that they always ended with O'Sullivan begging him to take his poor clittle, loving clittle, devoted clittle pet of a wife to a movie for a relaxation and a rest, or for a drink in the Russell, or to the evening races in the park; whereupon they would both hasten, panting, to Ferdy's flat to make love swiftly, wildly and vindictively – swiftly because their time was limited, wildly because her Irish storms had by now become typhoons of rage, and he no longer needed rose petals, Wagner, Mendelssohn, dim lights or pink champagne, and vindictively to declare and to crush their humiliation at being slaves to that idiot a quarter of a mile away in another bed saying endless rosaries to the Virgin.

Inevitably the afternoon came – it was now July – when Ferdy's pride and nerves cracked. He decided that enough was enough. They must escape to freedom. At once.

'Celia! If we have to fly to the end of the world! It won't really ruin my career. My master is most sympathetic. In fact since I hinted to him that I am in love with a *belle mariée* he does nothing but complain about his wife to me. And he can't leave her, his career depends on her, she is the daughter of a Secretary of State for Foreign Affairs – and rich. He tells me that at worst I would be moved off to someplace like Los Angeles or Reykjavik. Celia! My beloved flower! We could be as happy as two puppies in a basket in Iceland.'

She permitted a meed of Northern silence to create itself and then wondered reflectively if it is ever warm in Iceland, at which he pounced with a loud 'What do you mean? What are you actually asking? What is really in your mind?' She said, 'Nothing, dürling,' for how could she dare to say that whereas he could carry his silly job with him wherever he went she, to be with him, would have to give up her lovely old, friendly old boutique on the Green where her friends came to chat over morning coffee, where she met every rich tourist who visited Dublin, where she made nice money of her own, where she felt independent and free; just as she could never hope to make him understand why she simply could not just up and out and desert a dying husband.

'But there's nothing to hold you here. In his condition you'd be sure to get custody of the children. Apart from the holidays they could remain in school here the year round.'

So he had been thinking it all out. She stroked his hairy chest. 'I know.'

'The man, even at his best, you've acknowledged it yourself, over and over, is a fool. He is a moujik. He is a bore.'

'I know!' she groaned. 'Who should better know what a crasher he is? He is a child. He hasn't had a new idea in his head for thirty years. There have been times when I've hated the smell of him. He reminds me of an unemptied ashtray. Times when I've wished to God that a thief would break into the house some night and kill him. And,' at which point she began to weep on his tummy, 'I know now that there is only one thief who will come for him and he is so busy elsewhere that it will be years before he catches up with him. And then I think of the poor old bastard wetting his hospital bed, unable to stir, let alone talk, looking up at his ceiling, incontinent, with no scissors, no golf, no friends, no nothing, except me. How *can* I desert him?'

Ferdy clasped his hands behind his head, stared up at heaven's pure ceiling and heard her weeping like the summer rain licking his windowpane. He created a long Irish silence. He heard the city whispering. Far away. Farther away. And then not at all.

'And to think,' he said at last, 'that I once called you a realist!'

She considered this. She too no longer heard the muttering of the city's traffic.

'This is how the world is made,' she decided flatly.

'I presume,' he said briskly, 'that you do realize that all

Dublin knows that you are meanwhile betraying your beloved Meehawl with me?'

'I know that there's not one of those bitches who wouldn't give her left breast to be where I am at this moment.'

They got out of bed and began to dress.

'And, also meanwhile, I presume you do *not* know that they have a snotty name for you?'

'What name?' – and she turned her bare back for the knife.

'They call you The Diplomatic Hack.'

For five minutes neither of them spoke.

While he was stuffing his shirt into his trousers and she, dressed fully except for her frock, was patting her penny-brown hair into place before his mirror he said to her, 'Furthermore I suppose you do realize that whether I like it or not I shall one day be shifted to some other city in some other country. What would you do then? For once, just for once in your life tell me the plain truth! Just to bring you to the crunch. What would you really do then?'

She turned, comb in hand, leaned her behind against his dressing-table and looked him straight in the fly which he was still buttoning.

'Die,' she said flatly.

'That,' he said coldly, 'is a manner of speech. Even so, would you consider it an adequate conclusion to a love that we have so often said is forever?'

They were now side by side in the mirror, she tending her copper hair, he his black, like any long-married couple. She smiled a little sadly.

'Forever? Dürling, does love know that lovely word? You love me. I know it. I love you. You know it. We will always know it. People die but if you have ever loved them they are never gone. Apples fall from the tree but the tree never forgets its blossoms. Marriage is different. You remember the day he advised you that if you ever marry you should marry an Irishwoman. Don't, Ferdy! If you do she will stick to you forever. And you wouldn't really want that?' She lifted her frock from the back of a chair and stepped into it. 'Zip me up, dürling, will you? Even my awful husband. There must have been a time when I thought him attractive. We used to sail together. Play tennis together. He was very good at it. After all, I gave him two children. What's the date? They'll be home for the holidays soon. All I have left for him now is contempt and compassion. It is our bond.'

Bewildered he went to the window, buttoned his flowered waistcoat. He remembered from his café days as a student a ruffle of aphorisms about love and marriage. Marriage begins only when love ends. Love opens the door to Marriage and quietly steals away. *Il faut toujours s'appuyer sur les principes de l'amour – ils finissent par en ceder.* What would she say to that? Lean heavily on the principles of love – they will always conveniently crumple in the end. Marriage bestows on Love the tenderness due to a parting guest. Every *affaire de coeur* ends as a *mariage de convenance.* He turned to her, arranging his jacket, looking for his keys and his hat. She was peeking into her handbag, checking her purse for her keys and her lace handkerchief, gathering her gloves, giving a last glance at her hat. One of the things he liked about her was that she always wore a hat.

'You are not telling me the truth, Celia,' he said, quietly. 'Oh, I don't mean about loving me. I have no doubt about you on that score. But when you persuade yourself that you can't leave him because you feel compassion for him that is just your self-excuse for continuing a marriage that has its evident advantages.'

She smiled lovingly at him.

'Will you ring me tomorrow, dürling?'

'Of course.'

'I love you very much, dürling.'

'And I love you too.'

'Until tomorrow then.'

'Until tomorrow, dürling.'

As usual he let her go first.

That afternoon was some two years ago. Nine months after it he was transferred to Brussels. As often as he could wangle special leave of absence, and she could get a relative to stay for a week with her bedridden husband, now back in his own house, they would fly to Paris or London to be together again. He would always ask solicitously after her husband's health, and she always sigh and say his doctors had assured her that 'he will live forever.' Once, in Paris, passing a church he, for some reason, asked her if she ever went nowadays to confession. She waved the question away with a laugh, but later that afternoon he returned to it pertinaciously.

'Yes. Once a year.'

'Do you tell your priest about us?'

'I tell him that my husband is bedridden. That I am in love with another man. That we make love. And that I cannot give you up. As I can't, dürling.'

'And what does he say to that?'

'They all say the same. That it is an impasse. Only one dear old Jesuit gave me a grain of hope. He said that if I liked I could pray to God that my husband might die.'

'And have you so prayed?'

'Dürling, why should I?' she asked gaily, as she stroked the curly hair between his two pink buttons. 'As you once pointed out to me yourself all this was foreknown millions of years ago.'

He gazed at the ceiling. In her place, unbeliever though he was, he would, for love's sake, have prayed with passion. Not that she had said directly that she had not. Maybe she had? Two evasions in one sentence! It was all more than flesh and blood could bear. It was the Irish variation all over again: never let your left ass know what your right ass is doing. He decided to give her one more twirl. When she got home he wrote tenderly to her, 'You are the love of my life!' What she actually replied was, 'Don't I know it?' Six months later he had manoeuvred himself into the consular service and out of Europe to Los Angeles. He there consoled his broken heart with a handsome creature named Rosie O'Connor. Quizzed about his partiality for the Irish, he could only flap his hands and say, 'I don't know what they have got. They are awful liars. There isn't a grain of romance in them. And whether as wives or mistresses they are absolutely faithless!'

Something, Everything,
Anything, Nothing

1

Somebody once said that a good prime minister is a man who
knows something about everything and nothing about anything.
I wince – an American foreign correspondent, stationed in
Rome, covering Italy, Greece, Turkey, Corsica, Sardinia, Malta
Libya, Egypt and the entire Middle East.

Last year I was sent off to report on pollution around Capri,
steel in Taranto, which (as journalists say) 'nestles' under the
heel of the peninsula, the Italo-American project for un-
covering the buried city of the Sybarites, which is halfway
down the coast from Taranto, the political unrest then beginning to simmer in Reggio di Calabria, around the toe of the
continent, and, of course, if something else should turn up –
some 'extra dimension,' as my foreign editor in Chicago likes to
call such unforeseens . . .

Summer was dying in Rome, noisily and malodorously.
Down south, sun, silence and sea. It was such a welcome commission that it sounded like a pat on the head for past services. I
was very pleased.

I polished off Capri in two hours and Taranto in three days –
a well-documented subject. After lunching at Metaponto, now
one of Taranto's more scruffy seaside resorts, I was salubriously
driving along the highway beside the Ionian when, after about
an hour, 'something else' did crop up. It happened in a place too
minute to be called a village, or even a hamlet, an Italian would
call it a *loguccio* (a rough little place), named Bussano. I doubt
if many travellers, not natives of these parts of Calabria – bar-
ring Karl Baedeker some sixty years ago, or the modern
Italian Touring Club guide, or a weary Arab pedlar – had ever
voluntarily halted in Bussano. The Touring Club guide is eloquent about it. He says, and it is all he says: 'At this point the

29

road begins to traverse a series of monotonous sand dunes.' Any guide as reticent as that knows what he is not talking about.

Bussano consists of two lots of hovels facing one another across the highway, one backing on that wild stretch of the Calabrian Apennines called La Sila, the other on an always empty ocean; 'always' because there is no harbour south of Taranto for about a hundred and fifty miles, nothing but sand, reeds, a few rocks, the vast Ionian. I presume that during the winter months the Ionian Sea is often shaken by southwesterly gales. In the summer nothing happens behind those monotonous sand dunes except the wavelets moving a foot inward and a foot outward throughout the livelong day, so softly that you don't even hear their seesaw and you have to watch carefully to see their wet marks on sand so hot that it pales again as soon as it is touched. The *loguccio* looked empty.

The only reason I halted there was that I happened to notice among the few hovels on the sea side of the road one two-storeyed house with a line of brown and yellow sunflowers lining its faded grey-pink walls on which, high up, I could barely decipher the words *Albergo degli Sibariti*. The Sybarites' Hotel. It must have been built originally for travellers by stagecoach, first horse then motor, or by hired coach and horses, or by private carriage, or in later years by the little railroad along the coast that presently starts to worm its slow way up through those fierce mountains that climb seven thousand feet to the Serra Dolcedorme where, I have been told, snow may still be seen in May. It was the same friend who told me about a diminutive railroad in this deep south – could it be this one? – grandiosely calling itself *La Società Italiana per le Strade Ferrate del Mediterraneo–Roma*, five hundred miles from the smell of Rome and barred by the Apennines from the Mediterranean. The *Albergo degli Sibariti* would have flourished in the youth of Garibaldi.

I was about to move on when I glanced between the hotel and its nearest hovel at a segment of sea and horizon, teasingly evoking the wealth of centuries below that level line – Greece, Crete, Byzantium, Alexandria. Once again I was about to drive off, thinking how cruel and how clever of Mussolini, and also how economical, to have silenced his intellectual critics (men like, for instance, Carlo Levi) simply by exiling them to remote spots like this, when an odd-looking young man came through the wide passageway, halted and looked up and down the highway with the air of a man with nowhere to go and nothing to do.

He was dark, bearded and longhaired, handsome if you like mushy Italian eyes, dark as prunes, eyelashes soft and long, cheeks tenderly browned, under his chin hung a great, scarlet blob of tie like a nineteenth-century Romantic poet, his shirt gleaming (washed and ironed by whom?), his shoes brilliantly polished (by whom?), pants knife-pressed (by whom?), on his head a cracked and tawny straw hat that just might have come many years ago from Panama, and he carried a smooth cane with a brass knob. His unshaven jaws were blackberry blue. His jacket was black velvet. His trousers were purple. All in all more than overdressed for a region where the men may or may not wear a cotton singlet, but a shirt never except on Sundays, apart from the doctor if there is one, or the teacher if there is one, or the local landowner, and there is always one of them.

What on earth could he be? Not a visitor, at this time of the year, and in this non-place. An adolescent poet? More likely an absconding bank clerk in disguise. (Joke. In empty places like this the sand-hoppers for fifty miles around are known by their first names.) The local screwball? I alighted. He saw me. We met in the middle of the road – the roads down here are wide and fine. I asked him if he might be so kind as to tell me where I might, if it were not too much to ask, find the lost city of the Sybarites. At once he straightened his sagging back, replied eagerly, rapidly and excitedly, 'Three kilometres ahead fork left after the gas station then first right along a dirt track can I have a cigarette where are you from may I show you my pictures?'

Well, I thought, this is odd, I am on Forty-second Street, Division, Pigalle, the Cascine, the Veneto, Soho, Pompeii, show me his dirty pictures, what next? His sister? A pretty boy? Cannabis? American cigarettes? I told him I was an insurance salesman from Chicago and bade him lead on. He led me rapidly

31

through the passage to a wooden shack in the untidy yard behind the house, where, as he fumbled with the lock, he explained himself.

'I am a Roman I am a great painter I came down here two years ago to devote my life to my art I have been saving up for years for this a professor of fine arts from New York bought four of my paintings last week for fifty thousand lire apiece.'

I knew this last to be not so immediately he flung open the door on lines of paintings stacked around the earthen floor – there were three or four canvases but he had mostly used chipboard or plywood. His daubs all indicated the same subject, mustard yellow sunflowers against a blue sea, each of them a very long way after van Gogh, each the same greasy blob of brown and yellow, each executed (appropriate word!) in the same three primary colours straight from the tube, chrome yellow, burnt umber, cerulean blue, with, here and there as the fancy had taken him, a mix of the three in a hoarse green like a consumptive's spittle. They were the most supremely splendid, perfect, godawful examples of bad art I had ever seen. As I gazed at them in a Cortes silence I knew that I simply must possess one of them immediately.

Snobbery? A kinky metropolitan taste? I know the feeling too well not to know its source in compassion and terror. To me bad art is one of the most touching and frightening examples of self-delusion in the world. Bad actors, bad musicians, bad writers, bad painters, bad anything, and not just the in-betweeners or the borderliners but the total, desperate, irredeemable failures. Wherever I have come on an utterly bad picture I have wanted to run away from it or possess it as a work of horror. Those 'original' gilt-framed pictures in paper elbow guards displayed for sale in the foyers of big commercial hotels, or in big railroad terminals. A quarter of a mile of even worse 'originals' hanging from the railings of public parks in the summer. Those reproductions that form part of the regular stock of novelty stores that sell china cuckoo clocks, nutcrackers shaped like a woman's thighs, pepper pots shaped like ducks' bottoms. The poor, sad, pathetic little boy with the one, single, perfect teardrop glistening on his cheek. Six camels forever stalking across the desert into a red ink sunset. Three stretched-neck geese flying over a reedy lake into the dawn. That jolly medieval friar holding up his glass of supermarket port to an Elizabethan diamond-paned window as bright as a five-hundred-watt electric bulb.

We know the venal type who markets these *kitsch* objects and we know that they are bought by uneducated people of no taste. But if one accepts that these things are sometimes not utterly devoid of skill, and are on the edge of taste, who paints them? Looking into the earnest, globular eyes of this young man in Bussano (who insofar as he had no least skill and no least taste was the extreme example of the type) I felt once again the surge of compassion and of fear that is always the prelude to the only plausible answer I know: that he was yet another dreaming innocent who believed that he had heard the call to higher things. His type must be legion: young boys and girls who at some unlucky moment of their lives have heard, and alas have heeded that far-off whir of wings and that solitary midnight song once heard, so they have been told, in ancient days by emperor and clown, the same voice that flung magic casements open on the foam of perilous seas and faery lands forlorn. The frightening part of it is that there can be very few human beings who have not heard it in some form or another. If we are wise we either do nothing about it or do the least possible. We send a subscription, join something, vote, are modest.

As I offered him a cigarette I felt like the man in charge of a firing squad; not that I, or anybody else ever can kill such lethal innocence. As he virtually ate the cigarette I saw that his eye sockets were hollowed not by imagination but starvation. He was a living cartoon of the would-be artist as a young man who has begun to fear that he possibly may not be the one and will certainly never again be the other. To comfort him I irresponsibly said, 'You might one day become the van Gogh of Calabria,' to which he said quickly, 'I sell you any one you like cheap.' Should I have said they were all awful? I said I liked the one that, in characteristic burlesque of the real by the fake, he had labelled *Occhio d'oro, Mar' azzurro*. 'Golden Eye, Azure Sea.' Whereupon he said, 'Fifty dollars,' and I beat him down to two. As he pouched the two bills I asked him what he was proposing to do with all that lovely money. He laughed gaily – the Italian poor really are the most gutsy people in the world, as well as the most dream-deluded – 'Tonight I will bring my wife to the hotel for two brandies to celebrate my first sale in two years. It is an omen from heaven for our future.'

All this, and a wife too? I invited him into the hotel for a beer, served by a drowsy slut whom he had imperiously waked from her siesta. I asked him about his wife.

'Roman,' he said proudly. 'And *borghese*. Her father works in a bank. She believes absolutely in my future. When we married she said, "Sesto" – I was a sixth child, my name is Sesto Caro – "I will follow you to the end of the world." ' He crossed two fingers. 'We are like that.' He crossed three. 'With our child, like that. The first, alas, was stillborn.'

(The harm innocence can do!)

He said that he, also, was a Roman. And he was! He knew the city as well as I do, and I have spent twenty years living there as a nosy reporter. I found him in every way, his self-delusion apart, an honest young man. He agreed that he had done all sorts of things. Run away from home at fourteen. Done a year in the galleys for stealing scrap. Returned home, spent two years in a seminary trying to be a monk, a year and a half in a *trattoria* in the Borgo Pio. Was arrested again and held for two years without trial for allegedly selling cannabis. Released, he spent three years in Germany and Switzerland to make money for his present project. Returned home, was apprenticed as an electrician's assistant . . . He was now twenty-nine. She was now twenty-one. When she was turned off by her father they had come down here to beg the help of her godfather-uncle Emilio Ratti, an engineer living in what I heard him lightly call 'The Cosenza of Pliny and Varro.' I looked out and upwards towards the Sila.

'Cosenza? A godfather so far from Rome?'

'He was exiled there by Mussolini and never went back.'

Unfortunately, or by the whim of the pagan gods of Calabria – he contemptuously called it *Il Far Ovest* – his wife, then nineteen, and big with child, got diarrhoea so badly in Naples

('Pollution around Capri?') that they finally tumbled off the train at a mountainy place called Cassano in the hope of quickly finding a doctor there; only to be told as the train pulled away into the twilit valleys that the station of Cassano was hours away from the village of Cassano, whereas their informant, a carter from Bussano, offered to drive them in one hour to his beautiful village by the sea near which (equally untrue) there was a very good doctor. So, with their parcels, their cardboard suitcases, their paper bundles and bulging pillowcases they had come to this *casale* and stayed. Uncle Emilio had visited them once. Still, like her father, he occasionally disbursed small sums of money on condition that they stayed where they were.

2

We shook hands cordially, I gathered my bad painting and drove off fast. I had walked into the middle of a frightening story and I had no idea what its end would be. Murder? Suicide? If I could wait for either that could be a good something else for Chicago. Not now. No lift. No human interest. I looked eagerly ahead of me along the straight highway to my meeting with the skilled Italo-American technicians and archaeologists at Sybaris. About this, at least, van Gogh was accurate. After exactly three kilometres I saw the yellow and black sign of a gas station, whose attendant directed me, without interest, towards a dirt track leading into a marshland of reeds and scrub.

As I bumped along this dusty track I could see no life whatever, nothing but widespread swamp, until I came around a bend in the track and saw ahead of me a solitary figure leaning against a jeep, arms folded, pipe-smoking, well built, idly watching me approach. High boots to his knees, riding breeches, open-necked khaki shirt, peaked cap, sunglasses, grizzled hair. In his sixties? I pulled up beside him, told him who and what I was and asked him where I could see the buried city of Sybaris. Immobile he listened to me, smiled tolerantly, or it might be boredly, then without speaking beckoned me with his pipe to follow his jeep. I did so until he halted near a large pool of clear water surrounded by reeds and mud. Some ten feet underwater I perceived a couple of broken pillars and a wide half-moon of networked brick.

'Behold Sybaris,' he said and with amusement watched me stare at him, around the level swamp at the immensity of the all-seeing mountains and back to him again.

'You mean that's *all* there is to see of it?'

'All, since, if you believe the common legend, its enemies deflected its great river, the Crathis,' he in turn glanced westwards and upwards, 'to drown it under water as Pompeii was smothered in volcanic ash. Crathis is now brown with yellow mud. "Crathis the lovely stream that stains dark hair bright gold." '

He smiled apologetically at the quotation.

'But the archaeologists? I was hoping to find them all hard at work.'

He smiled unapologetically. He relit his pipe.

'Where is the hurry? Sybaris has been asleep a long time. They have finished for this year. They have had to work slowly. They have been experimenting with sonic soundings since 1964. They have had to map the entire extent of the city with their magnetometers. It was six miles in circumference. But I am only an engineer. Consultant engineer. Of Cosenza.'

I stared unhappily at the solitary eye of the once largest and most elegant city of the whole empire of Magna Graecia. I recalled and mentioned an odd detail that had stuck in my mind's tooth, out of, I think, Lenormant, supposedly typical of the luxury of the city in its heyday – its bylaw that forbade morning cocks to crow earlier than a stated number of hours after sunrise. He shrugged dubiously. I did know that it was Lenormant who a hundred years ago looked from the foothills of the Sila down at this plain and saw nothing but strayed bulls, long since gone wild, splashing whitely in its marshes. He said he had been much struck by this legendary picture.

'Legendary? You *are* a sceptical man.'

'In this country legend is always posturing as history. We are a wilderness of myths growing out of myths. Along the coast there, at Crotone, my wife, as a girl, walked to the temple of Juno, the Mother of the Gods, in a procession of barefooted girls singing hymns to Mary, the Mother of God. Here Venus can overnight become Saint Venus. *Santa Venera.* A hill once sacred to Cybele becomes sanctified all over again as Monte Vergine. I do not deride any of this. Some myths point to a truth. Some not. I cannot always distinguish. And I have lived in Calabria for thirty years.'

'Not a born Calabrese, then?'

'I am a Roman. I was exiled here by the Fascisti in 1939. Not in this spot! Back up there in a small village called San Giovanni in Fiore. A pretty name, situated beautifully, poor and filthy when you got there. The night they arrested me in Rome they allowed me five minutes and one suitcase. I grabbed the biggest book I could find. It was *Don Quixote.* That winter I reread it by daylight and by candlelight three times. I had nothing else to read, nobody to talk to, nothing to do. Every fine day I tramped over those mountains, sometimes twenty and more miles a day.' He laughed cheerfully. 'Wearing out the Fascist spies detailed to follow me. Today the same men, as old as I am now, joke with me over it. They were bastards every one of them. And would be again if it suited them. They say, "Ah, the good old days, Emilio! You were so good for our bellies. If only we could lead one another that dance all over again!" I came everywhere on old stories written on old stones – myths, charms, omens, hopes, ambitions. The cerecloths of Greece. The marks of Rome. Those bits in that pool are probably Roman. You can tell it by the *opus reticulatum* of the bricks. That was only uncovered in '32. They call this place the *Parco del Cavallo.* What horse? Whose horse? I came on remnants of Byzantium, the Goths, the Saracens, the Normans. Our past. When my spies saw what I was after they stopped following me – I had become a harmless fool – doors opened to me, a landowner's, then a doctor's, even a schoolmaster's, a learned priest's in Rossano. I met and fell in love with a doctor's daughter from Crotone. It was a charming little port in those days. Good wine of Ciro. Good cigars. Very appealing. One day in September 1943 the British Fifth Army entered Crotone and we were married. Well before then,' he laughed, 'every Fascist of San Giovanni in Fiore had burned his black shirt and started shouting *Viva il Re*. The old woman with whom I had lodged sold me for two thousand lire to the doctor, who sold me for twenty thousand to the police marshal, who sold me for fifty thousand to a landowner who drove me into Crotone to show the British commanding officer the victim of Fascism whom he had protected for the last four years. I did not give him away. I had fallen in love so much with Calabria that I even liked its ruffians. I settled in Cosenza.'

Why was he unburdening himself like this to a stranger? I said that in Sptember 1943 I was with the American Eighth Army across those mountains.

'My God!' I wailed, throwing a bit of silver wrap from my chewing gum into the pool of the horse. 'Do you realize that all that is over a quarter of a century ago?'

He smiled his tender, stoic's smile.

'I realize it very well. My younger son is a lieutenant in the Air Force. His brother is studying medicine in Palermo. My eldest child is due to have her first baby at any hour.'

'Why did you not return to Rome?'

He again glanced towards Cosenza. The sun, I observed, sinks early behind those Apennines. For no reason there flashed across my eyes the image of this plain covered by sheets of water made of melting snow.

'I have told you why I never went back to Rome. Because I had fallen in love with a woman and a place, with a woman who was a place. I saw my Claudia as a symbol of the ancientness, the ancestry, the dignity, the unforgettable beauty of Calabria, of its pedigree, its pride, its arrogance, its closeness to the beginning of the beginnings of man and the end of the ends of life. I believed then and believe still that outside Calabria it would be impossible to find such a woman as my Claudia.'

I did not suggest that fifty million Italians might not agree. If a young man in love, and an old man remembering his young love is not entitled to his dreams, who is? I merely suggested that there is also some 'ancientness' in Rome.

'In museums? In Rome the bridge is down. It has no living

past. It is just as venal, vulgar, cowardly, cynical and commercial a city as any other in the world.' He jerked his body to a soldierly attention. 'I must get back to Cosenza. We have been warned by the doctor that the birth may be difficult. There may have to be a caesarian. My wife will be praying for an easy birth. When I get back she may have more news.'

No relatives? Ageing both. Alone. I did not say that my own daughter has married far away from me into another continent. All dreams have an ending somewhat different from their beginnings.

'Your daughter is in Cosenza?' I asked hopefully, but he waved his right hand towards the south.

'No. She married a splendid young man in Reggio, an *avvocato*. Bartolomeo Vivarini. It is not very far but it is far too far for my wife and me at a time like this.'

We shook hands warmly. We had in some way lit in those few minutes a small flame to friendship. He waved and went his way. I continued along the coast, deeper into his South, his beloved Past.

I slept in Crotone, badly, woke wondering if I had been as unwise about my food as one so easily can be anywhere south of Rome, or dreamed oppressively, or failed to do something along the road that I ought to have done. It was not until I had dived into the sparkles of the sea and been driving fast for a good hour that the reason for my dejection struck me. I had caught the *mal du pays*. Four days out of Rome and I was already homesick for it. And why not? I am not married to Old Calabria. I am a political animal, a man of reason, interested in the world as it really is. My job is to do with today, occasionally with tomorrow, never with yesterday. I had been seeing far too many memorials to that incorporeal, extramundane, immaterial, miasmic element that is food and drink to men like Emilio Ratti and that Carl Sandburg called a bucket of ashes.

One ancient temple had been exciting, like those fifteen Doric columns at Metaponto deep in weeds and wild flowers. The next, less than a mile away, had been too much. A cartload of stones. Decline, decay, even death is Beauty's due. Never defeat. This South is littered with decay and defeat. Farther on a bare few megaliths recorded another defeated city. A duck pond to call up great Sybaris! Not even a stone had marked another lost city. Juno's great church had been worn by time, weather and robbery to a naked column on the edge of a bleak moor and a bare cliff outside Crotone. All as empty now as the sea, except for ageing women remembering the garlanded girls who once walked there in a line singing hymns in May. At Locri I had paused for gas and found the local museum ill-kept and dusty. *Aranciata Pitagora.* One of Greece's greatest philosophers advertising orange juice over a wayside stall.

I covered my final forty miles in half an hour. I swept into a Reggio bristling with carabinieri, local police, armed troops, riot squad trucks crackling out constant radio reports. The hotel was like a Field H.Q. with pressmen and photographers, cinema crews and TV crews. All because it was widely and furiously feared that Rome intended to pass Reggio over in favour of either Cosenza or Catanzaro as the new provincial capital. Posters all over the walls announced that at four o'clock there would be a Monster Meeting in the Piazza del Popolo. This would leave me just enough time to interview the chief citizens of Reggio: mayor, archbishop, city councillors, parliamentary deputies, labour bosses, leading industrialists if any. For some five hours, lunchless, I patiently gathered from them thousands of flat-footed words, to which at the afternoon meeting a sequence of bellowing orators added their many more.

Weary, hungry and bored I remembered with a click of my fingers the name Vivarini.

3

Twenty minutes later, in a quarter of the city far removed from the noisy piazza, I was admitted by an elderly woman in black – wife? housekeeper? secretary? – to the presence of a very old man in a dusky room cluttered with antiquated furniture, bibelots, statuettes in marble, alabaster and bronze, old paintings, vases, boxes of papers, books, bowls, crystal paperweights, signed photographs in silver frames. It was the kind of room that made me wonder how he ever found anything he might require there. A Balzac would have been delighted to list all its telltale signs, markers or milestones of the fortunes of a business and a family, especially those signed photographs – King Vittorio Emmanuele III, Dr Axel Munthe, one Peter Rothschild, Prime Minister Giolitti (the one who held out against Mussolini until 1921), Facta (who fell to Fascism in 1922), Mussolini's son-in-law Galeazzo Ciano, Marshal Badoglio. As for me, one look and I knew what I was in for. And I was!

'Ah, *signore*, this was once a city of the rarest elegance. My son whom you must meet – he is at the hospital – does not realize this, he is too young. But I myself heard d'Annunzio say that our *lungomare* is one of the most gracious seaside promenades in Europe. What do you think of that?' (I refused to say that if the so-called Prince of Montevenoso ever said so he must have said it before 1908 when this city was flattened by its terrible earthquake, and at that date Signor Vivarini would have been a very small boy indeed.) 'But, now, alas, *signore*, we have been taken over by the vulgar herd, the *popolazzo*. Corruption. Vendettas. Squabbles for gain. Maladministration. And all because our natural leaders, our aristocracy, the landed gentry of Calabria, started to abandon Reggio immediately after the earthquake of 1908 . . .'

In the distance an irritable rattle of rifle fire. He did not seem to hear it. He went on and on. And I should be back there at the rioting.

'Nothing can save us now but a miracle . . . When I was a youth . . .'

I rose at the sound of a distant, dull explosion, ready to run from him without ceremony, when from the doorway I found myself transfixed by the stare of a man whom I took to be his son – a tall, thin, challenging, cadaverous man of about thirty-five, eyes Atlantic grey, peering through eyelashes that hid nothing of his patent awareness of his own merits, his inquisitorial mistrust, his cold arrogance of a pasha. I would have been utterly repelled by him if his clothes were not so much at odds with his manner. His lean body was gloved in a light, metallic, bluish material suggestive of shimmering night and

41

stars, his skintight shirt was salmon pink, his lemon tie disappeared into the V of a flowered waistcoat, the silk handkerchief in his breast pocket lolled as softly as a kitten's tail, or as its eyes, his shoes were sea-suede, and his smoke of hair was blued like a woman's. After all those big mouths in the piazza he looked so promisingly ambiguous that I introduced myself at once, name, profession, nationality. In a courteous and attractively purring voice, and in the unmistakable English of Cambridge (Mass.), i.e., of Harvard, he replied that he had also spent some time in America. In return I told him that I had begun my career as a journalist on *The Crimson*. His laugh was loud, frank, open and delighted. We shook hands amiably. I was on the point of deciding that he was really a most engaging fellow when I recalled his first ice-cold air, his arrogance and his suspicion. I glanced at his clothes and I looked at his face, where now it was the mouth that impressed me: a blend of the soft, the mobile, the vulpine, the voracious, the smiling that made me suddenly think that the essence of his first effect on me had been the predatory and the self-protective nature of a born sensualist. Obviously a man capable of being very attractive to women, but also, I feared, capable in his egoism of being cruel.

'You enjoyed America,' I stated cheerfully.

For a second or two his peering mask returned and he smiled, not unhappily, yet not warmly either, the way I fancied an inquisitor might when watching a heretic slowly gyrating over the flames that would soon deliver his soul to paradise. He said that he had endured the arid rigidities of Harvard University for three years. He laughed gaily at another rattle of gunfire, saying, 'That nonsense will be over in an hour.' He did not so much invite me to dine with him, as insist that I should give him the pleasure.

'And the consolation. I am going through a difficult time.'

The next second he was blazing with fury at his father's tremulous question, 'How is Angelica?' This – I had observed in some embarrassment – had already been iterated four times.

'She has been in labour now for eight hours!' he ground out savagely. 'If she has not given birth within three more hours I insist upon a caesarian.' The old man waved protesting hands.

'My dear father!' he raged at him in a near whisper. 'I have told you twenty times that there is nothing scientifically wrong with a caesarian.'

He turned suavely to me. 'I do wish my dear father would realize that even after three caesarians my wife could still bear him a long line of grandchildren.' He laughed lightly. 'Of course there is no truth in the legend that Julius Caesar was so delivered. I will call for you at your hotel – The Excelsior I presume? – at half past seven. We will dine at the Conti. It is not very much but it is our best.'

I would have preferred to catch the plane for Rome. But I remembered, and shared, some of Emilio Ratti's quiet trouble-ment over his daughter. My own daughter had not had an easy time with her first. There bounced off my mind the thought that a nameless young woman in Bussano had lost her first. Actually it was none of these things decided me but the sound of more shots. I ran from the pair of them.

The rioting was well worth it, water cannon, baton charges, rubber bullets, the lot, women howling Jesu Marias, hair streaming, children bawling, fat men behaving like heroes, the finest fullest crop of De Sica clichés, vintage 1950, and not a cat killed. And all for what? For, at least, more than Hecuba, if for less than Hector. For pride, honour, family, home, ancient tradition, *Rhegium antiquum* so often raped by Messinaians, Syracusans, Romans, Goths, Normans, Saracens, Pisans, Turks, Aragonese, Fascisti, Nazis, and the liberating armies of Great Britain and the U.S.A. Also, no doubt, for something to do with real estate, tourism, air travel, emigration, IRI, Bernie Cornfield's *fonditalia*, Swiss hooks in Chiasso, the Mafia, the *Cassa per il Mezzogiorno*, the Demochristians' majority in par-liament ... But the journalist's classical symptom is cynicism, the boil of his inward frustration, the knowledge that he will never get at that total truth reserved for historians, novelists and poets who will reduce his tormented futilities to a few drops of wisdom.

By the time Vivarini called for me I was calmed, and if apart from Crotone's morning moonshine coffee still unfed, I was by now not unslaked, braced by two martinis which I insisted that he and I, at the bar, make four; as, in Conti's he at once ordered not one but two litres of *vino di Ciro* – reminding me of that drunken night, it was in Peking (Oh! Jesus!) years and years ago, that I first became a father.

'No!' he groaned aloud to the totally empty restaurant (Its usual clients afraid to emerge at night?) 'No baby yet!'

His father ('Don't touch the *scampi*! Even here we have possible pollution!') was a Polonius, a foolish, fond old man whom nobody would mistake for his better, three generations out of date. A sweet, kind man. With fine sensibilities. But, like all Italians, a besotted sentimentalist.

'By comparison I, Bartolomeo . . .'

'Hi, Bart! Call me Tom!'

'Hi, Tom . . . am a cold Cartesian. My wife,' he informed me secretively, evidently making some point, 'is a mortal angel. I have selected her with the greatest care. For I have also had my sorrows. My betrayals. But she is an angel with a Gallic mind. She also loathes all this traditional nonsense of her father's and of my father, all this ridiculous adoration of the Past. Down with Tradition! All it is is confusion! Mythology! Obfuscation!' He hammered the table, a waiter came running and was dismissed. 'I insist on a caesarian! Those two old men with their folksy minds think it bad, wrong, a threat to the long line of children they dream of as their – *their!* – descendants. Excuse me,' he said quietly. 'May I telephone?'

He returned, swaying only a very little, shook his head, looked at his watch, while I thought of my engineer and his wife waiting by the telephone in Cosenza, and that agonized girl hauling on a towel tied to the end of a bedpost, and the old lawyer somewhere up the street moaning to himself among his portraits and his trophies of the dead and I said, 'Look't, for Chrissake, forget me! I know you want to be back in that hospital, or nursing home, or whatever it is. Do please go there!' – to which, intent on behaving as calmly as a Harvard man, that is to say as a Yank, that is to say as an English gentleman (period 1850) would have behaved, he replied that if his papa was irrational his father-in-law Emilio was far more so.

'I can guess how my father explained those riots to you. The decay of the aristocracy? All that shit? But did he once mention the Mafia? With whom, of course, he worked hand in glove all his life? Whereas, on the other hand, Emilio would know all about the Mafia, but he would also tell you that the rioting would have been far worse if it had not been for,' here one could almost hear his liver gurgling bile, 'the "wisely restraining hand of Mother Church." Two complementary types of total unreason.'

At this he bowed his face into his palms and moaned into them.

'If only my love and I could get out of this antiquated, priest-ridden, Mafia-ridden, time-ridden, phony, provincial hole!'

He quickly recovered control of himself sufficiently to beg me, concernedly, to give him the latest news from the States. I did so, keeping it up as long and lightly as I could since the narration seemed to soothe him. But it was only a seeming, because he suddenly cried out, having obviously not heeded one word I had been saying:

'The Church here is, of course, a master plotter and conspirator. Have you seen their latest miracle?' – as if he were asking me whether I had seen the latest Stock Exchange reports. 'You must. It is a masterpiece. It is only five hundred metres away. A weeping Madonna. Weeping, of course, for Reggio. Like Niobe, from whom the idea most certainly derives. What a gullible people we are! Madonnas who weep, bleed, speak, go pale, blush, sway, for all I know dance. Did you know that before the war Naples possessed two bottles of milk supposed to have been drawn off the breasts of the Virgin which curdled twice a year? Excuse me. May I telephone?'

He disappeared. This made the restaurant twice as empty. The patron asked me solicitously if all was well. Signor Vivarini seemed upset? I said his wife was expecting a baby.

'A baby!'

Within a minute the restaurant came alive. A fat female cook bustled from the kitchen. After her came a serving woman. The *padrone's* wife appeared. Two small children peeped. An old man shuffled out in slippers. In a group they babbled about babies. It was nine o'clock. I had lost my plane. I had not yet written my report on Reggio. But he did not come back and he did not come back, and I was cross, bothered, bored and bewildered. The restaurant again emptied – the whole company of family and servitors had gone off in a gabble to regather outside the telephone booth. I had decided to pay the bill and leave when a mini-riot burst into the place, all of them returning, cheering and laughing, to me, as if I was the fertile father, and in their midst Bartolomeo Vivarini, swollen as the sun at noon, beaming, triumphant, bestowing benedictions all around, proclaiming victory as smugly as if he was the fertile mother.

'*Un miracolo gradito!*' he laughed and wept, 'a son! I am the father of a son! I have telephoned my father and my mother, my father-in-law and my mother-in-law. They are all such good people. Are they not?'

The company laughed, clapped, declared that it was indeed a miracle, a splendid miracle, a *miracolo gradito*.

'There will be more children!' the cook assured him.

'And more sons,' the *padrone*'s father assured him.

He sat, sobbed, hiccuped, called for champagne, but this I firmly forbade.

'You haven't yet seen your wife!' I pointed out. 'She must have suffered terrible pain,' at which his sobs spouted like champagne.

'I had forgotten all about her!' he wailed and punished his bony breast. 'I must light a candle for my wife to the Madonna. To the weeping Madonna! Let us go, my dear friend. To the Madonna! She, perhaps, may make them give me one peep at my son. You will drive me? I dare not! It is not far away.'

So, we left, led noisily by all to the door. And nobody asked us to pay the bill.

His car was a Lancia. I drove it furiously to somewhere up the hill, this way, that way, until, above the nightness and lightness of the city, of the straits, of all Calabria and all Sicily, we halted on the edge of a tiny *piazza* crowded with worshippers or sightseers, where there stood an altar, and on the altar a pink and blue commercial statue of the allegedly lachrymose Virgin Mary. A hundred breathless candles adored her, and four steady electric spotlights. Bartolomeo crushed me through the crowds to the altar, bought two candles, one for himself, one for me, refusing to take any change from his thousand-lire bill, lit his candle, fixed it in position and knelt on the bare ground to pray, his hands held wide in total wonder and belief.

As far as I was concerned the miracle was, of course, like every popular Italian miracle preposterous – a word, I had learned at high school, that means in Ciceronian Latin arse-to-front. The object was to me simply an object, bought from some statue vendor in Reggio, with, if even that ever happened, a drop or two of glycerine deposited on its painted cheek by some pious or impious hand. But why should anybody want a miracle so badly, and gradually, as I looked about me and felt the intensity of the human feeling circling the altar like a whirl-pool of air, or bees in a swarm, or butterflies over a wave, or fallen leaves whispering in a dry wind, I began to feel awed and even a little frightened. As I moved through the murmuring or silent crowds, conscious of the eloquent adoration of the old, the unexpected fervour of the young, the sudden hysteria of a woman carried away screaming, the quiet insistent stare of two Franciscans fixed on the painted face, I became so affected that at one point I thought that I, too, could, might, perhaps – or did I? – see one single, perfect teardrop gleaming in the spotlights on the face of the mother of their God. I blinked. 'It' vanished.

But had it ever been there? Who had the proof that it had not been an illusion for us all? The night was inflammable, the country explosive, I had too much respect for my skin to ask why even one teardrop had not been looked at through a mi-croscope capable of distinguishing between glycerine, that is to say $C_3H_5(OH)_3$ and the secretions of the lachrymal gland. I might as well have committed instant suicide as suggest that a similar test could be applied to the wine said to change during their Mass into the blood of their God. I found myself beside the two motionless friars. I cautiously asked one of them if he had seen, or knew anybody who had seen, a tear form in the Madonna's eye. He answered skilfully that this was not wholly relevant since if one saw the tear it was so, and if one did not see a tear it was not so, which he took pleasure in explaining to me courteously, but at some length, marks the difference in Kantian philosophy between the *phenomenon* and the *noumenon*. My mind swam.

Bartolomeo had vanished. I stayed on in that haunted *piaz-zetta* until well after one in the morning. I collected some opinions, two asserted experiences, stories of miraculous cures. The crowds thinned, but at no time was the statue unattended by at least one worshipping believer. Only when a palsied dumb woman asked me the time by tapping my watch with her finger did I remember that by now the huntsmen might be asleep in Calabria but the foreign editors of America would be wide awake, for who could be drowsy at that hour whose first edition frees us all from everlasting sleep? A few steps away I found a lighted café whose owner must have nourished the same views as Sir Thomas Browne. There, over a couple of Stregas, I disposed in twenty minutes of Reggio's political troubles. Inside another half an hour I evoked the miracle of the Madonna in one of the most brilliant pieces I have written during my whole life. The best part of it was the coda, which I doubted I would ever send – they would only kill it at once. In it I asked Chicago, still daylit, still dining or well dined, rumbling like old thunder, smelling as rank as a blown-out candle, how it is that the Mediterranean never ceases to offer us new lamps for old. I opined that it is because it is in the nature of that restless Mediterranean mind to be divinely discontent with this jail of a world into which we are born. It is always trying to break out, to blow down the walls of its eyes, to extend time to eternity so as to see this world as nobody except the gods has ever seen it before.

No! Not for Chicago. Not that I cared. What is every journalist anyway but an artist *manqué* spancelled to another, who is tethered to a third, and a fourth and a fifth up to the fiftieth and final *manqué* at the top?

I passed slowly back through the little *piazza*. The candles were guttering, the spotlights still shone, it was empty except for one man kneeling in the centre of it before the sleepless statue. I bade her a silent farewell, Juno, Hera, Niobe, Venus, or the Virgin, and went on walking through the sleeping streets down-hill to the shore. It was a still night. The sky gleamed with stars like Vivarini's blue coat. I thought of my dauber of Bussano, my van Gogh *manqué*, and I decided that the distinction between Emperor and Clown is irrelevant. Every virtue is woven into its opposite, failure built into ambition, despair into desire, cold reason into hot dreams, delusion into the imagination, death into life, and if a youth does not take the risks of every one of them he will not live long enough to deserve peace.

I paused. In the straits was that a purring motorboat? Not a sound. Here, at about five twenty o'clock one equally silent morning sixty-one years ago – it was in fact December 28th – people like the father and mother of old Mr Vivarini the lawyer felt their houses sway and shiver for thirty-two seconds, and for twelve miles north and south every house swayed and shook in the same way for two months. At widening intervals the earthquake went on for a year and a half. The entire city vanished. Like Sybaris. Like Pompeii. I looked at my watch. In a few hours another green sheen would creep over the straits. Another pallid pre-morning lightsomeness would expand behind Aspromonte.

I walked on smiling at the fun the Vivarinis would have disputing over the name of their newborn child.

An Inside Outside Complex

So then, a dusky Sunday afternoon in Bray at a quarter to five o'clock, lighting up time at five fifteen, November 1st, All Souls' Eve, dedicated to the suffering souls in Purgatory, Bertie Bolger, bachelor, aged forty-one or so, tubby, ruddy, greying, well-known as a dealer in antiques, less well-known as a conflator thereof, walking briskly along the seafront, head up to the damp breezes, turns smartly into the lounge of the Imperial Hotel for a hot toddy, singing in a soldierly basso 'my breast expanding to the ball.'

The room, lofty, widespread, Victorian, gilded, over-furnished, as empty as the ocean, and not warm. The single fire is small and smouldering. Bertie presses the bell for service, divests himself of his bowler, his vicuna overcoat, his lengthy scarf striped in black, red, green and white, the colours of Trinity College, Dublin (which he has never attended), sits in a chintzy armchair before the fire, pokes it into a blaze, leans back, and is at once invaded by a clearcut knowledge of what month it is, and an uneasy feeling about its date. He might earlier have adverted to both if he had not, during his perambulation, been preoccupied with the problem of how to transform a twentieth-century Buhl cabinet, now in his possession, into an eighteenth-century ditto that might plausibly be attributed to the original M. Boulle. This preoccupation had permitted him to glance at, but not to observe, either the red gasometer by the harbour inflated to its winter zenith, or the haybarn beside the dairy beyond the gasometer packed with cubes of hay, or the fuel yard, facing the haybarn, beside the dairy beyond the gasometer, heavily stocked with mountainettes of coal, or the many vacancy signs in the lodging houses along the seafront, or the hoardings on the pagoda below the promenade where his mother, God rest her, had once told him he had been wheeled as a coiffed baby in a white pram to hear Mike Nono singing 'I do liuke to be besiude the seasiude, I do liuke to be besiude the sea,' or, most affectingly of all, if he had only heeded them, the exquisite, dying leaves of the hydrangeas in the public gardens, pale green, pale yellow, frost white, spiking the air above once purple petals that now clink greyly in the breeze like tiny seashells.

He suddenly jerks his head upright, sniffing desolation, looks slowly about the lounge, locates in a corner of it some hydrangeas left standing too long in a brass pot of unchanged water, catapults himself from the chair with a 'Jaysus! Five years to the bloody day!', dons his coat, his comforter and his bowler hat, and exits rapidly to make inland towards the R.C. church. For days after she died the house had retained that rank funereal smell. Tomorrow morning a Mass must be said for the repose of his mother's soul, still, maybe – Who knows? Only God knows! – suffering in the flames of Purgatory.

It is the perfect and pitiless testing date, day and hour for any seaside town in these northern islands. A week or two earlier and there might still have been a few lingering visitors, a ghost of summer's lukewarmth, a calmer sea, unheard waves, and, the hands of the Summer Time clocks not yet put backwards, another hour of daylight. This expiring Sunday the light is dim, the silence heavy, the town turned in on itself. As he walks through the side avenues between the sea and the Main Street, past rows of squat bungalows, every garden drooping, past grenadiers of red brick, lace curtained, past ancient cement-faced cottages with sagging roofs, he is informed by every fanlight, oblong or halfmoon, blank as night or distantly lit from the recesses behind each front door, that there is some kind of life asleep or snoozing behind number 51, *Saint Anthony's, Liljoe's, Fatima,* 59 (odd numbers on this side), *The Billows, Swan Lake,* 67, *Slievemish, Sea View,* names in white paint, numbers in adhesive celluloid. Every one of them gives a chuck to the noose of loneliness about his neck. I live in Dublin. I am a guest in a guest house. I am Mister Bee. I lunch of weekdays at the United Services Club. I dine at the Yacht Club.

Good for biz. Bad for Sundays, restaurants shut, homeless. Pray for the soul of Mrs Mary Bolger, of Tureenlahan, County Tipperary, departed this life five years ago. Into thy hands, O Lord.

On these side avenues only an odd front window is lit. Their lights flow searingly across little patches of grass called front gardens, privet-hedged, lonicera-hedged, mass-concrete hedged. Private. Keep Off.

As he passed one such light, in what a real estate agent would have called a picture window, he was so shaken by what he saw inside that after he had passed he halted, looked cautiously about him, turned and walked slowly back to peep in again. What had gripped his attention through the unsuspecting window had been a standing lamp in brass with a large pink shade, and beneath its red glow, seated in an armchair with her knees crossed, a bare-armed woman reading a folded magazine, one hand blindly lifting a teacup from a Moorish side table, holding the cup immobile while she concentrated on something that had detained her interest. By the time he had returned she was sipping from the cup. He watched her lay it down, throw the magazine aside and loop forward on two broad knees to poke the fire. Her arms looked strong. She was full-breasted. She had dark hair. In that instant B.B. became a *voyeur*.

The long avenue suddenly sprang its public lights. Startled he looked up and down the empty perspective. It was too cold for evening strollers. He was aware that he was trembling with fear. He did not know what else he was feeling except that there was nothing sexy to it. To calm himself he drew back behind the pillar of her garden gate whose name plate caught his eye. *Lorelei*. He again peeped around the side of the pillar. She was dusting her lap with her two palms. She was very dark, a western type, a Spanish-Galway type, a bit heavy. He could not discern the details of the room beyond the circle of light from the pink lamp, and he was glad of this: it made everything more mysterious, removed, suggestive, as if he was watching a scene on a stage. His loneliness left him, his desolation, his longing. He wanted only to be inside there, safe, secure, and satisfied.

'Ah, good evening, Bertie!' she cried to the handsome man who entered her room with the calm smile of complete sang-froid. 'I am so glad, Bertie, you dropped in on me. Do tell me your news, darling. How is the antique business? Come and warm your poor, dear hands. It is going to be a shivering night. Won't you take off your coat? Tea? No? What about a drink? I know exactly what you want, my pet. I will fix it for you. I have been waiting and waiting for you to come all the livelong day, melting with longing and love.'

As he gently closed the door of the cosy little room she proffered her hand in a queenly manner, whereupon our hero, as was fitting, leaned over it – because you never really do kiss a lady's hand, you merely breathe over it – and watched her eyes asking him to sit opposite her.

The woman rose, took her tea tray, and the room was suddenly empty. Her toe hooked the door all but a few inches short of shut. He was just as pleased whether she was in the room or out of it. All he wanted was to be inside her room. As he stared, her naked arm came slowly back into the room between the door and the jamb, groping for the light switch. A plain gold bangle hung from the wrist. The jamb dragged back the shoulder of her blouse so that he saw the dark hair of her armpit. The window went black.

He let out a long, whistling breath like a safety valve and resumed his long perambulation until he saw a similar light streaming from the window of an identical bungalow well ahead of him on the opposite side of the roadway. He padded rapidly towards it. As he reached its identical square cement gate-pillars he halted, looked backwards and forwards and then guardedly advanced a tortoise nose beyond the edge of the pillar to peep into the room. A pale, dawnlike radiance, softly tasselled, hinted at comfortable shapes, a sofa, small occasional chairs, a pouffe, a bookcase, heavy gleams of what could be silver, or could be just electroplated nickel. Here, too, a few tongues of fire. In the centre of the room a tall, thin, elderly man in a yellow cardigan, but not wearing a jacket or tie, stood so close beside a young girl with a blonde waterfall of hair as to form with her a single unanalysable shape. He seemed to be speaking. He stroked her smooth poll. They were like a still image out of a silent film. They were presumably doing something simple, natural and intimate. But what? They drew apart abruptly and the girl, while stooping to pick up some shining object from a low table, looked in the same movement straight out through the window. B.B. was so taken by surprise that he could not stir, even when she came close to the window, looked up at the sky, right and left, as if to see if it was raining, turned back, laughed inaudibly, waved the small silver scissors in her hand.

In that instant, at that gesture, some time after five fifteen on the afternoon of November 1st, the town darkening, the sky lowering, his life passing, a vast illumination broke like a sunrise upon his soul. At the shut-time of the year all small towns become smaller and smaller, dwindle from out-of-doors to in-of-doors; from long beaches, black roads, green fields, wide sun, to kitchens, living-rooms, bedrooms, locked doors, drawn blinds, whispers, prayers, muffling blankets, nose-hollowed pillows; from making to mending; to littler and littler things, like this blonde Rapunzel with a scissors and a needle; all ending in daydreaming, and nightdreaming, and dreamless sleeping. How pleasant life could be in that declension to a white arm creeping between a door and a jamb, bare but for a circle of gold about a wrist and a worn wedding ring on one heavy finger. But I am outside. When the town is asleep in one another's arms I will sleep under the walls. No wife. No child. Mister Bee.

The headlamps of a motorcar sent him scurrying down an unlighted lane that may once have led to the mews of tall houses long since levelled to make room for these hundreds of little bungalows. In this abandoned lane the only window-light was one tiny, lofty aperture in the inverted V of a gable rising like a castle out of tall trees. Below it, at eye level the lane was becoming pitch dark. Above it, a sift of tattered light between mourning clouds. Hissing darkness. A sheaving wind. The elms were spiky as if the earth's hair was standing on end. He stiffened. A bird's croak? A sleepless nest? A far-off bark? He stared up at the tiny box of light whose inaccessibility was so much part of its incitement that when it went black like a fallen candle he uttered a 'Ha!' of delight. He would never know who had put a finger on the switch of that floating room. A maidservant about to emerge into the town? To go where? To meet whom? A boy's den? An old woman lumbering down the long stairs?

That Monday morning B.B. was laughing happily at himself. Bertie Bolger, the well-known dealer! The Peeping Tom from Tipperary! That was a queer bloody fit I took! And Jaysus, I forgot all about the mother again: well, she will have to wait until next year now though surely to God they'll let her out before then? Anyway, what harm did she ever do bar that snibby way she treated every girl I ever met; if it wasn't for her I might have been married twenty years ago to that Raven girl I met in 1950 in Arklow. And a hot piece she was, too . . . Mad for it!

The next Sunday evening he was padding softly around the back roads of Bray. He could not locate the old-man-blonde-girl bungalow. He winked up at the little cube of light. But *Lorelei* was dark. The next two Sundays were raining too heavily for prowling. On the fourth Sunday the window of *Lorelei* was brilliantly lighted, and there she was plying a large dressmaker's scissors on some coloured stuff laid across a gate-legged table under the bare electric bulb whose brightness diminished the ideality of the room, increased the attractions of the dressmaker. Broad cheekbones, like a Red Indian; raven hair; the jerky head of a blackbird alert at a drinking pool. He longed to touch one of those fingers, broad at the tip like a little spade. Twice the lights of an oncoming car made him walk swiftly away, bowler hat down on nose, collar up. A third time he fled from light pouring out of the door of the adjacent bungalow and a woman hurrying down its path with her overcoat over her head and shoulders. Loping away fast he turned in fright to the running feet behind him and saw her coat-ends vanish under the suddenly lighted door lamp of *Lorelei*. Damn! A visitor. Spoiling it all. Yet, he came back to his watching post, as mesmerized as a man in a vast portrait gallery who returns again and again to *Portrait of Unknown Woman*, unable to tell why this one unidentified face makes him so happy. The intruder, he found, made no difference to his pleasure.

'Jenny! Isn't that a ring at the door? Who the divil can that be?'

'I bet that will be Mrs Ennis from next door, she promised to give me a hand with these curtains, you don't mind, darling, do you?'

'Mind! I'm glad you have friends, Molly.'

'Hoho! I've lots of friends.'

'Boyfriends, Katey?'

'Go 'long with you, you ruffian, don't you ever think of anything but the one thing?'

'Can you blame me with a lovely creature like you, Peggy, to be there teasin' me all day long, don't stir, I'll let her in.'

In? To what? There might be a husband and a pack of kids, and at once he had to sell his *Portrait of Unknown Woman* for the known model, not being the sort of artist who sees a new face below his window, runs out, drags her in, and without as much as asking her name spends months searching for her inner reality on his canvas.

Every Sunday he kept coming back and back to that appealing, rose-pink window until one afternoon, when he saw her again at her tea, watched her for a while, and then boldly clanged her black gate wide open, boldly strode up her path, leaped up three steps to her door, rang her bell. A soft rain had begun to sink over the town. The day was gone. A far grumble of waves from the shingle. She opened the door. So close, so solid, so near, so real he could barely recognize her. His silence made her lift her head sideways in three slow, interrogatory jerks. She had a slight squint, which he would later consider one of her most enchanting accomplishments – she might have been looking at another man behind his shoulder. He felt the excitement of the hunter at her vulnerable nearness. He suddenly smelled her. Somebody had told him you can always tell a woman's age by her scent. *Chanel* – and Weil's *Antelope* – over sixty. *Tweed* – always a mature woman. *Madame Rochas* – the forties. The thirties smell of after-shave lotion: *Eau Sauvage*, *Mustache*. Wisps of man scent. The twenties – nothing. She had a heavy smell. Tartly she demanded, 'Yes?' Unable to speak, he produced his business card, handed it to her spade fingers. *Herbert Bolger/ Antiques/ 2 Hume Street, Dublin.* She laughed at him.

'Mister Bolger, if you are trying to buy something from me I have nothing, if you are trying to sell me something I have even less.'

He was on home ground now, they all said that, he expected it, he relied on them to say it. His whole technique of buying depended on knowing that while it is true that the so-called Big Houses of Ireland have been gleaned by the antique dealers, a lot of Big House people have been reduced to small discouraged houses like this one, bringing with them, like wartime refugees, their few remaining heirlooms. Her accent, however, was not a Big House accent. It was the accent of a workaday country-woman. She would have nothing to sell.

'Come now, Mrs Eh? Benson? Well, now, Mrs Benson, you say you have nothing to sell but in my experience a lot of people don't know what they have. Only last week I paid a lady thirty pounds for a silver Georgian saltcellar that she never knew she possessed. You might have much more than you realize.'

He must get her alone, inside. He had had no chance to see her figure. Her hair shone like jet beads. Her skin was not a flat white. It was a lovely, rich, ivory skin, as fine as lawn or silk. He felt the rain on the back of his neck and turned up his coat collar. He felt so keyed up by her that if she touched him his string would break. She possessed one thing that she did not know about. Herself.

'Well, it is true that my late husband used to attend auctions. But.'

'Mrs Benson, may I have just one quick glance at your living-room?' She wavered. They always did. He smiled reassuringly. 'Just one quick glance. It will take me two minutes.'

She looked up at the rain sifting down about her door lamp.

'Well? Alright then ... But you are wasting your time. I assure you! And I am very busy.'

Walking behind her in the narrow hallway, he took her in

from calves to head. She was two women: heavy above, lighter below. He liked her long strong legs, the wide shoulders, the action of her lean haunches, and the way her head rose above her broad shoulders. Inside, the room was rain-dim, and hour-dim, until she switched on a central hundred-and-fifty-watt bulb that drowned the soft pink of the standing lamp, showed the furniture in all its nakedness, exposed all the random marks and signs of a room that had been long lived in.

At once he regretted that he had come. He walked to the window and looked out through its small bay up and down the avenue. How appealing it was out there! All those cosy little, dozing little, rosy little bungalows up and down the avenue, these dark trees comforting the gabled house with its one cube of light, and, her window being slightly raised above the avenue, he could see the scattered window of other cosy little houses coming awake all over the town. An hour earlier he might have been able to see the bruise-blue line of the Irish Sea. I could live in any one of those little houses out there, and he turned to look at her uncertainly – like a painter turning from easel to model, from model to easel, wondering which was the concoction and which was the truth.

'Well?' she asked impatiently.

His eye helicoptered over her cheap furniture. Ten seconds sufficed. He looked at her coldly. If he were outside there now on the pavement, looking in at her rosy lamp lighting . . .

'There is,' she said defensively, 'a mirror.'

She opened the leaves of large folding doors in the rear wall, led him into the room beyond them, flooded it with light. An electric sewing machine, patterns askew on the wall, a long deal table strewn with scattered bits of material, a tailoress's wire dummy and, incongruously, over the empty fireplace, a lavish baroque mirror, deeply bevelled, sunk in a swarm of golden fruit and flowers, carved wood and moulded gesso. Spanish? Italian? It could be English. It might, rarest of all, be Irish. Not a year less than two hundred years old. He flung his arms up to it.

'And you said you had nothing! She's a beauty! I'd be delighted to buy this pretty bauble from you.'

She sighed at herself in her mirror.

'I did not say I have nothing, Mr Bolger. I said I have nothing for you. My mirror is not for sale. It was my husband's engagement present to me. He bought it at an auction in an old house in Wexford. It was the only object of any interest in the house, so there were no dealers present. He got it for five pounds.'

He darted to it through an envious groan. He talked at her through it.

'Structurally? Fine. A leaf missing here. A rose gone there. Some scoundrel has dotted it here and there with commercial gold paint. And somebody has done worse. Somebody's been cleaning it. Look here and here and here at the white gesso coming through the gold leaf. It could cost a hundred pounds of gold leaf to do it all over again. Have you,' he said sharply to her in the mirror, 'been cleaning it?'

'I confess I tried. But I stopped when I saw that chalky stuff coming through. I did, honestly.'

He considered her avidly in the frame. So appealing in her contrition, a fallen Eve. He turned to her behind him. How strongly built and bold she was! Bold as brass. Soft as silk. No question – *two* women!

'Mrs Benson, have you any idea what this mirror is worth?'

She hooted at him derisively.

'Three times what you would offer as a buyer, and three times that again for what you would ask as a seller.'

He concealed his delight in her toughness. He made a sad face. He sighed heavily.

'Lady! Nobody trusts poor old B.B. But you don't know how the game goes. I look at that mirror and I say to myself, "How long will I wait to get how much for it?" I say, "Price, one hundred pounds," and I sell it inside a month. I say, "Price, two hundred pounds," and I have to wait six months. Think of my overheads for six months! If I were living in London and I said, "Price, three hundred pounds," I'd sell it inside a week. If I lived in New York, I could say, "Price fifteen hundred dollars," and I'd sell it in a day. If I lived on a coral island it wouldn't be worth two coconuts. That mirror has no absolute value. To you it's priceless because it has memories. I respect you for that, Mrs Benson. What's life without memories? I'll give you ninety pounds for it.'

They were side by side, in her mirror, in her room, in her life. He could see her still smiling at him. Pretending she was sorry she had cleaned it! Putting it on! They do, yeh know, they do! And they change, oho, they change. Catch her being sorry for anything. Smiling now like a girl caught in fragrant delight. Listen to this:

'It is not for sale, Mr Bolger. My memories are not on the market. That is not a mirror. It is a picture. The day my husband bought it we stood side by side and he said,' she laughed at him in the mirror, ' "We're not a bad looking pair." '

He stepped sidewards out of her memories, keeping her framed.

'I'll give you a hundred quid for it. I couldn't possibly sell it for more than a hundred and fifty pounds. There aren't that many people in Dublin who know the value of a mirror like yours. The most I can make is twenty-five per cent. You are a dressmaker. Don't you count on making twenty-five per cent? Where are you from?' he asked, pointing eagerly.

'I'm a Ryan from Tipperary,' she laughed, taken by his eagerness, laughing the louder when he cried (untruthfully) that he was a Tipp man himself.

'Then you are no true Tipperary woman if you don't make fifty per cent! What about it? Tipp to Tipp. A hundred guineas? A hundred and ten guineas? Going, going . . .?'

'It is not for sale,' she said with a clipped finality. 'It is my husband's mirror. It is our mirror. It will always be our mirror,' and he surrendered to the memory she was staring at.

As she closed the door on his departure there passed between them the smiles of equal strangers who, in other circumstances, might have been equal friends. He walked away, exhilarated, completely satisfied. He had got rid of his fancy. She had not come up to his dream. He was cured.

The next Sunday afternoon, bowler hat on nose, collar up, scarfed, standing askew behind her pillar, the red lamp glowing, will now always glow above the dark head of Mrs Benson, widow, hard-pressed dressmaker, born in Tipperary, sipping Indian tea, munching an English biscuit, reading a paperback, her civil respite from tedious labour. How appealing! She has beaten a cosy path of habit that he lusts to have, own, at least to share with her. 'I can make antiques but I can't make age, I could buy the most worn bloody old house in Ireland and I wouldn't own one minute of its walls, trees, stones, moss, slates, gravel, rust, lichen, ageing.' And he remembered the old lady in a stinking dry-rotted house in Westmeath, filled with eighteenth-century stuff honeycombed by woodworm, who would not sell him as much as a snuffbox because, 'Mister Bulgey, there is not a pebble in my garden but has its story.'

Bray. For sale. Small modern bungalow. Fully furnished. View of sea. Complete with ample widow attached to the front doorknob. Fingerprints alive all over the house.

He pushed the gate open, smartly leaped her steps, rang.

A fleck of biscuit clung childishly to her lower lip. Her grey eye, delicately defective, floated beyond his face as disconcertingly as a thought across surprise.

'Not you again!' she laughed lavishly.

'Mrs Bee! I have a proposition.'

'Mister Bee! I do not intend to sell you my mirror. Ever!'

'Missus Bee! I do not want your mirror. What I have to propose will take exactly two tics. I swear it. And then I fly.'

She sighed, looked far, far away. Out over the night sea?

'For two minutes? Very well. But not *one* second more!'

She showed him into the living-room and, weakening – in the name of hospitality? of Tipperary? of old country ways? – she goes into the recesses of her home for an extra cup. In sole possession of her interior he looks out under the vast umbrella of the dusk, out over the punctured encampment of roofs. Could I live here? Why does this bloody room never look the same inside and outside? Live *here*? Always? It would be remote. Morning train to Dublin. In the evenings, this, when I had tarted it up a bit, made it as cosy, lit inside, as it looks from the outside.

'My husband,' she said, pouring, 'always liked China tea. You don't mind?'

'I am very partial to it. It appeals to my aesthetic sense. Jasmine flowers. May I ask what your husband used to do?'

'Ken was an assessor for an English insurance company. He was English.'

He approved mightily, fingers widespread, chin enthusiastically nodding.

'A fine profession! A very fine profession!'

'So fine,' she said wryly, 'that he took out a policy on his own life for a bare one thousand pounds. And I am now a dressmaker.'

'Family?' he asked tenderly.

She smiled softly.

'My daughter, Leslie. She is at a boarding school. I am hoping to send her to the university. What is your proposition?'

Her profile, soft as a seaflower, changed to the obtuseness of a deathmask, until, frontally, its lower lip caught the light, the eyes became alert, the face hard with character.

'It is a simple little proposition. Your mirror, we agree, is a splendid object, but for your business quite unsuitable. Any woman looking into it can only half see herself. What you need is a great, wide, large, gilt-framed mirror, pinned flat against the wall, clear as crystal, a real professional job, where a lady can see herself from top to toe twirling and turning like a ballet dancer.' He smiled mockingly. 'Give your clients status.' He proceeded earnestly. 'Worth another two hundred pounds a year to you. You would be employing two assistants in no time. I happen to have a mirror just like that in my showrooms. I've had it for six years and nobody has wanted it.' He paused, smiling from jawbone to jawbone. 'I would like you to take it. As a gift.'

Shrewdly he watched her turning her teacup between her palms as if she were warming a brandy glass, while she observed him sidewards just as shrewdly out of an eye as fully circled as a bird's. At last she smiled, laid down her cup, leaned back and said, 'Go on, Mr B.'

'How do you mean, "go on"?'

'You have only told me half your proposition. You want something in return?'

He laughed with his throat, teeth, tongue and gullet, enjoying her hugely.

'Not really!'

She laughed, enjoying him as hugely.

'Meaning?'

He rose, walked to the window, now one of those black mirrors that painters use to eliminate colour in order to reveal design. The night had blotted out everything except an impression of two or three pale hydrangea leaves wavering outside in the December wind and, inside, himself and a lampshade. He began to feel that he had already taken up residence here. He turned to the woman looking at him coldly under eyebrows as heavy as two dark moustaches and flew into rage at her resistance.

'Dammit! Can't you give me credit for wanting to give you something for your own sake?' As quickly he calmed. The proud animal was staring timidly, humbly, contritely. Or was she having him on again? She could hide anything behind that lovely squint of hers. He demanded abruptly, 'Do you ever go into Dublin?'

She glanced at the doors of her workroom.

'I must go there tomorrow morning to buy some linings. Why?'

'Tomorrow I have to deliver a small Regency chest to a lady in Greystones. On my way back I could call for you here at ten o'clock, drive you into Dublin and show you that big mirror of mine, and you can take it or leave it, as you like.' He got up to go. 'Okay?'

She gave an unwilling assent but as she opened the front door to let him out added, 'Though I am not at all sure that I entirely understand you, Mister B.'

'Aren't you?' he asked with an impish animation.

'No, I am not!' she said crossly. 'Not at all sure.'

Halfway across her ten feet of garden he turned and laughed derisively. 'Have a look at the surface of your mirror,' and twanged out and was lost in a dusk of sea-fog.

She returned slowly to her workroom. She approached her mirror and peered over its surface. Flawless. Not a breath of dust. With one spittled finger she removed a flyspeck. What did the silly little man mean? Without being aware of what she was doing she looked at herself, patted her hair in place, smoothed her fringe, arranged the shoulder peaks of her blouse, then, her dark eyebrows floating, her bistre eyelids sinking, her back straight, her bosom lifted, she drawled, 'I really am afraid, Mister B., that I still do *not* at all understand you,' and chuckled at the effect. Her jaw shot out, she glared furiously at her double, she silently mouthed the word, 'Fathead!' seized her scissors and returned energetically to work. She would fix him! Tomorrow morning she would let the ten o'clock train take her to Dublin.

He took her to Dublin, and to lunch, and to her amused satisfaction admitted that there was a second part to his proposition. He sometimes persuaded the owners of better class country hotels to allow him to leave one or two of his antiques, with his card attached, on view in their public rooms. It could be a Dutch landscape, or a tidy piece of Sheraton or Hepplewhite. Free advertisement for him, free decor for them. Would she like to co-operate? 'Where on earth,' some well-off client would say, 'did you get that lovely thing?' – and she would say, 'Bolger's Antiques.' She was so pleased to have foreseen that there would be some such *quid pro quo* that she swallowed the bait. So, the next Sunday, though he did not bring his big mirror, he brought a charming Boucher fire screen. The following Sunday his van was out of order, but he did bring a handsome pair of twisted Georgian candlesticks for her mantelpiece. Every Sunday, except during the Christmas holidays when he did not care to face her daughter, Leslie, he brought something: a carved, bronze chariot, Empire style, containing a clock, a neat Nelson sideboard, a copper warming pan, so that they always had something to discuss over their afternoon tea. It amused and pleased her until the day came when he produced a pair of (he swore) genuine Tudor curtains for her front window and she could no longer conceal from herself that she was being formally courted, and that her living-room had meanwhile been transformed from what it had been four months ago.

The climax came at Easter when, for Leslie's sake, she weakly allowed him to present her with two plane tickets for a Paris holiday. In addition he promised to visit her bungalow every day and sleep there every night while she was away. On her return she found that he had left a comic 'Welcome Home' card on her hall table; that her living-room was sweet with mimosa; that he had covered her old-fashioned wallpaper with (he explained) a hand painted French paper in (she would observe) a pattern of Nôtre Dame, the Eiffel Tower, the Arc de Triomphe and the Opéra; replaced her old threadworn carpet – she and Ken had bought it nearly twenty years ago in Clery's in O'Connell Street – by (he alleged) a *quali* Persian carpet three hundred years old; and exchanged her central plastic electric shade for (he mentioned) a Waterford cluster. In fact he had got rid of every scrap of her life except her mirror, which now hung over her fireplace, her pink lamp and, she said it to herself, 'Me?'

The next Sunday she let him in, sat opposite him, and was just about to say her rehearsed bit of gallows humour – 'I am sorry to have to tell you, Bertie, that I don't particularly like your life, may I have mine back again please?' – when she saw him looking radiantly at her, realized that by accepting so many disguised gifts she had put herself in a false position, and burst into tears of shame and rage. Bertie, whose many years of servitude with his mother had made all female tears seem as ludicrous as a baby's squealing face, laughed boomingly at her, enchanted to see this powerful woman so completely in his power. The experience filled him with such joy that he sank on his knees beside her, flung his arms about her, and said, 'Maisie, will you marry me?' She drew back her fist, gave him such a clout on the jaw that he fell on his poll, shouted at him, 'Get up, you worm! And get out!'

With hauteur he went.

She held out against him for six months, though still permitting him to visit her every Sunday for afternoon tea and a chat. In November, without warning, her resistance gave out. Worn down by his persistence? Or her own calculations? By her ambitions for Leslie? Perhaps by weariness of the flesh at the prospect of a life of dressmaking? Certainly by none of the hopes, dreams, illusions, fears and needs that might have pressed other hard-pressed women into holy wedlock; above all not by the desires of the flesh – these she had never felt for Bertie Bolger.

He made it a lavish wedding, which she did not dislike; he also made it showy, which she did not like; but she was soon to find that he did everything to excess, including eating, always defending himself by the plea that if a man or a woman is any good you cannot have too much of them; a principle that ought to have led him to marry the Fat Lady in the circus, or led her to marry Paddy O'Brien, the Irish giant, who was nine feet high and whose skeleton she had once seen preserved in the College of Surgeons. 'Is he all swank and bluff?' she wondered. Even on their honeymoon she discovered that after a day of boasting about his prowess compared with all his competitors, it was ten to one that he would either be crying on her shoulder long past midnight, or yelping like a puppy in one of his nightmares; both of which performances (her word) she bore with patience until the morning he dared to give her dogs' abuse for being the sole cause of all of them, whereat she ripped him with a kick like a cassowary. She read an article about exhibitionism. That was him! She read a thriller about a manic-depressive strangler, and peeping cautiously across the pillows, felt that she should never go to bed with him without a pair of antique duelling pistols under her side of the mattress.

Within six months they both knew that their error was so plenary, so total, so irreducible that it should have been beyond speech – as it was not. He said that he felt a prisoner in this bloody bungalow of hers. He said that whenever he stood inside her window (and his Tudor curtains) and looked out at those hundreds of lovely, loving, kindly, warm, glowing, little peaked bungalows outside there he knew that he had picked the only goddam one of the whole frigging lot that was totally uninhabitable. She said she had been as free as the wind until he took forcible possession of her property and filled it with his fake junk. He said she was a bully. She told him he was a bluffer. He said, 'I thought you had brains but I've eaten better.' She said, 'You're a dreamer!' He said, 'You're a dressmaker!' She said, 'You don't know from one minute to the next whether you want to be Jesus Christ or Napoleon.' He shouted, 'Outside the four walls of this bungalow you're an ignoramus, apart from what little I've been able to teach you.' She said, 'Outside your business, Bertie Bolger, and that doesn't bear close examination, if I gave you three minutes to tell me all *you* know, it would be six minutes too much.' All of it as meaningless and unjust as every marital quarrel since Adam and Eve began to bawl with one voice, 'But *you* said . . .,' and 'I know what *I* said, but you said . . .' 'Yes but then *you* said . . .'

His older, her more recent club acquaintances chewed a clearer cud. At the common table I once heard three or four of them mentioning him over lunch. They said next to nothing but their tone was enough. Another of those waxwork effigies that manage somehow or other to get past the little black ball into the most select clubs. Mimes, mimics, fair imitations, plausible impersonations of The Real Thing, a procession of puppets, a march of masks, a covey of cozens, a levee of liars: chaps for whom conversation means anecdotes, altruism alms, discipline suppression, justice calling in the police, pleasure puking in the washroom, pride swank, love lust, honesty guilt, religion fear, patriotism greed and success cash. But if you asked any of those old members to say any of this about Bertie? They would look you straight in the top button of your weskit and say, without humour, 'A white man.' And Maisie? 'A very nice little wife.'

Dear Jesus! Is life in all clubs reduced like this to white men and nice little wives? Sometimes to worse. As well as clubbites there are clubesses to whom the truth is told between the sheets and by whom enlarged, exaggerated, falsified, and spread wide. After all, the men had merely kicked the testicles of his reputation; the wives castrated him. They took Maisie's part. A fine, natural countrywoman, they said; honest as the daylight; warm as toast if you did not cross her, and then she could handle her tongue like the tail end of a whip; a woman who carried her liquor like a man; as agile at Contract as a trout; could have mothered ten and would never give one to Bertie, whom she had let marry her only because she saw he was the sort of weakling who always wants somebody to lean on, and did not find out until too late that he was miles away from what every woman really wants, which is somebody she can rely on. Their judgement made him seem much less than he was, her much more. The result of it was that he was soon feeling the cold wind of Dublin's whispering gallery on his neck and had to do something to assert himself unless he was to fall dead under the sting of its mockery.

Accordingly, one Sunday afternoon in November, a year after his marriage, he packed two suitcases, called a cab, and drove off down the lighted avenue to resume his not unimportant role in life as the Mister Bee of some lonely guest house. It had not, at the end been her wish. If she had not grown a little fond of him she had begun to feel a little sorry for him. Besides, next autumn Leslie would be down on her fingers and up on her toes at the starting line for the university, waiting eagerly for the revolver's flat 'Go!'

'This is silly, Bertie!' she had shrugged as they heard and saw the taxi pulling up outside their window. 'Husbands and wives always quarrel.' He picked up his two suitcases and looked around the room at his lost illusions, a Prospero leaving for the mainland. 'It's nothing unusual,' she had said, to comfort him. 'It happens in every house,' she had pleaded, 'But they carry on.'

'You bitch!' he had snarled, making for the door. 'You broke my heart. I thought you were perfect.'

She need not have winced, knowing well that they had both married for reasons the heart knows nothing of. Nevertheless she had gone gloomily into her dining-room, which must again become her workroom. The sixty pounds that he had agreed to pay her henceforth every month, though much more than she had had before they met, would not support two people. Looking about it she noted, with annoyance, that she had never got that big mirror out of him.

So then, a dusky Sunday afternoon in Bray, at a quarter to five o'clock, lighting up time five fifteen, All Souls' Eve, dedicated to the souls of the dead suffering in the fires of Purgatory,

Bertie Bolger, half Benedict half bachelor, aged forty-four, tubby, ruddy, greying, walking sedately along the seafront, sees ahead of him the Imperial Hotel and stops dead, remembering.

'I wonder!' he wonders, and leaning over the promenade's railings, sky-blue with orange knobs, rusting to death since the nineteenth century, looks down at the damp pebbles of the beach. 'How is she doing these days?' and turns smartly inland towards the town.

At this ambiguous hour few houses in Bray show lighted windows. The season is over, the Sunday silent, landladies once more reckoning their takings, snoozing, thinking of minute repairs, or praying, in *Liljoe's, Fatima, The Billows, Swan Lake, Sea View*. Peering ahead of him Mr B. sees, away down the avenue, a calm glow from a window and feels thereat the first, delicate, subcutaneous tingle that he has so often felt in the presence of some desirable object whose value the owner does not know. Nor does he know why those rare lighted windows are so troubling, suggestive, inviting, rejecting, familiar, foreign, like any childhood's nonesuch, griffin, mermaid, unicorn, hippogriff, dragon, centaur, crested castle in the mountains where there grows the golden rose of the world's end. Not knowing, he ignores that first far-off glow, turns from it as from a temptation to sin, turns right, turns left, walks faster and faster as from pursuing danger, until his head begins to swim and his heart to drumroll at the sight, along the perspective of another avenue, of a lighted roseate window that he knows he knows.

As he comes near to *Lorelei* he looks carefully around him to be sure that he is not observed by some filthy Paul Pry who might remember him from that year of his so-called marriage. He slows his pace. He slowly stalks the pillar of his wife's house. He peeps inside and straightway has to lean against the pillar to steady himself, feeling his old dream begin to swell and swell, his old disturbance mount, fear and joy invade his blood at the sight of her seated before the fire, placid, self-absorbed, her teacup in her hand, her eyes on her book, the pink glow on her threequarter face, more than ever appealing, inciting, sealed, bonded, unattainable.

I *have* neglected her. I owe her restitution. He enters the garden, twangs the gate, mounts the steps, rings the bell, turns to see the dark enfold the town. A scatter of lights. The breathing of the waves. The glow of a bus zooming up Kilruddery Hill a mile away, lighting the low clouds, bare trees, passing the Earl of Meath's broken walls, his gateway's squat Egyptian pillars bearing, in raised lettering, the outdated motto of his line, LABOR VITA MEA.

'Bertie!'

'Maisie!'

'I'm so glad you dropped in, Bertie. Come in. Take your coat off and draw up to the fire. It's going to be a shivering night. Let me fix you a drink. The usual, I suppose?' Her back to him: 'As a matter of fact I've been expecting you every Sunday. I've been waiting and waiting for you.' She laughed. 'Or do you expect me to say I've been longing and longing for you since you abandoned me last November?'

He looks out, shading his eyes, sees the window opposite light up. They, too, have a pink lampshade.

'That,' he said, 'is the Naughtons' bungalow, isn't it? It looks very cosy. Very nice. I sometimes used to think I'd be happy living there, looking across at you.'

She glances at it, handing him the whiskey, sits facing him, pokes the fire ablaze.

'We're all alike, in our bungalows. Why did you come today, Bertie?'

'It's our marriage anniversary. I didn't know what gift to send you, so I thought I would just ask. Hello! Your mirror is gone!'

'I had to put it back in my workroom. If you want to give me a present give me your mirror.'

'Jesus, I never did give it to you, did I? Next Sunday, I swear! Cross my heart! I'll bring it out without fail. If the van is free.'

In this easy way they chatted of this and that, and he went on his way, and he came back the next Sunday, though not with his mirror, and he came every Sunday month after month for tea or a drink. On his fourth visit she produced, for his greater comfort, an old pair of felt slippers he had left behind him, and on the fifth Sunday a pipe of his that she had discovered at the bottom of a drawer. He did not come around Christmas, feeling that Leslie would prefer to be alone with her mother. Instead he spent it at the Imperial Hotel. In a blue paper hat? She refused to let him send them both to Paris for Easter but she did let him send Leslie. For her own Easter present she asked, 'Could I possibly have that mirror, Bertie?' – and he promised it, and did not keep his promise, saying that someday she would be sure to give up dressmaking and not need it, and anyway he was somehow getting attached to the old thing, it would leave a big pale blank on his wall if he gave it away, and after all she had a mirror of her own, but he promised, nevertheless, that he would sometime give it to her.

The music of the steam carousel played on the front, the town became gay, English tourists strolled up and down the lapis lazuli and orange promenade, voices carried, and now and again he went for a swim before calling on her, until imperceptibly it was autumn again, with the rainy light fading at half past four and her rosy window appealing to him to come inside, and in her mirror he would tidy his windblown hair and his tie, and look in puzzlement around the room, and speculatively back at her behind him pouring his drink, just as if he were her husband and this was really his home, so that it was a full year again, and November, and All Souls' Eve before she saw him drive up outside her gate, accompanied by his man Scofield, in his pale blue-and-pink van, marked along its side in Gothic silver lettering, BOLGER'S ANTIQUES, and, protruding from it his big mirror, wrapped in felt and burlap. She greeted it from her steps with a mock cheer that died when Scofield's eye flitted from the mirror to her door, and from door back to mirror, and Bertie's did the same, and hers did the same, and they all three knew at once that his mirror was too big for her. Still, they tried, until the three of them were standing in a row in her garden looking at themselves in it where it leaned against the tall privet hedge lining the avenue, a cold wind cooking the sweat on their foreheads.

'I suppose,' Bertie said, 'we could cut the bloody thing up! Or down!' – and remembering one of those many elegant, useless,

disconnected things he had learned at school from the Ben-
edictines, he quoted from the Psalms the words of Christ about
the soldiers on Calvary dicing for his garments: '*Diviserunt sibi
vestimenta mea et super vestem maem miserunt sortem.*'

'Go on!' he interpreted. 'Cut me frigging shirt in bits and play
cards for me jacket and me pants,' which was the sign for her to
lead him gently indoors and make three boiling hot toddies for
their shivering bones.

He was silent as he drank his first dram, and his second. After
the third dram he said, okay, this was it, he would never come
here again, moving with her and Scofield to the window to look
at his bright defeat leaning against the rampant hedge of privet.

And, behold, it was glowing with the rosiness of the window
and the three of them out there looking in at themselves from
under the falling darkness and the wilderness of stars over town
and sea, a vision so unlikely, disturbing, appealing, inviting,
promising, demanding, enlisting that he swept her to him and
held her so long, so close, so tight that the next he heard was the
pink-and-blue van driving away down the avenue. He turned
for reassurance to the gleaming testimony in the garden and
cried, 'We'll leave it there always! It makes everything more
real!' At which, as well she might, she burst into laughter at the
sight of him staring out at himself staring in.

'You bloody loon!' she began, and stopped.

She had heard country tales about people who have seen on
the still surface of a well, not their own hungry eyes but the
staring eyes of love.

'If that *is* what you really want,' she said quietly, and kissed
him, and looked out at them both looking in.

Murder at Cobbler's Hulk

It takes about an hour of driving southwards out of Dublin to arrive at the small seaside village of Greystones. (For two months in the summer, it calls itself a resort.) Every day, four commuter trains from the city stop here and turn back, as if dismayed by the sight of the desolate beach of shingle that stretches beyond it for twelve unbroken miles. A single line, rarely used, continues the railway beside this beach, on and on, so close to the sea that in bad winters the waves pound in across the track, sometimes blocking it for days on end with heaps of gravel, uprooted sleepers, warped rails. When this happens, the repair gangs have a dreary time of it. No shelter from the wind and spray. Nothing to be seen inland but reedy fields, an occasional farmhouse or abandoned manor, a few leafless trees decaying in the arid soil or fallen sideways. And, always, endless fleets of clouds sailing away towards the zinc-blue horizon.

Once there were three more tiny railway stations along these twelve miles of beach, each approached by a long lane leading from the inland carriage road to the sea. The best preserved of what remains of them is called Cobbler's Hulk. From a distance, one might still mistake it for a real station. Close up, one finds only a boarded waiting room whose tin roof lifts and squeaks in the wind, a lofty signal cabin with every window broken and a still loftier telephone pole whose ten crossbars must once have carried at least twenty lines and now bear only one humming wire. There is a rotting, backless bench. You could scythe the grass on the platform. The liveliest thing here is an advertisement on enamelled sheet metal, high up on the brick wall of the signal cabin. It showed the single white word STEPHEN'S splashed across a crazy blob of black ink. Look where one will, there is not a farmhouse nor cottage within sight.

It was down here that I first met Mr Bodkin one Sunday afternoon last July. He was sitting straight up on the bench, bowler-hatted, clad, in spite of the warmth of the day, in a well-brushed blue chesterfield with concealed buttons and a neatly tailored velvet half collar that was the height of fashion in the Twenties. His grey spats were as tight as gloves across his insteps. He was a smallish man. His stiff shirt collar was as high as the Duke of Wellington's, his bow tie was polka-dotted, his white moustaches were brushed up like a Junker's. He could have been seventy-three. His cheeks were as pink as a baby's bottom. His palms lay crossed on the handle of a rolled umbrella, he had a neatly folded newspaper under his arm, his patent-leather shoe tips gleamed like his pince-nez. Normally, I would have given him a polite 'Good day to you' and passed on, wondering. Coming on him suddenly around the corner of the waiting room, his head lowered towards his left shoulder as if he were listening for an approaching train, I was so taken by surprise that I said, 'Are you waiting for a train?'

'Good gracious!' he said, in equal surprise. 'A train has not stopped here since the Bronze Age. Didn't you know?'

I gazed at his shining toes, remembering that when I had halted my Morris Minor beside the level-crossing gates at the end of the lane, there had been no other car parked there. Had he walked here? That brambled lane was a mile long. He peeked at the billycan in my hand, guessed that I was proposing to brew myself a cup of tea after my solitary swim, chirruped in imitation of a parrot, 'Any water?' rose and, in the comic-basso voice of a weary museum guide, said, 'This way, please.' I let him lead me along the platform, past the old brass faucet that I had used on my few previous visits to Cobbler's Hulk, towards a black-tarred railway carriage hidden below the marshy side of the track. He pointed the ferrule of his umbrella.

'My chalet,' he said smugly. 'My *wagon-lit*.'

We descended from the platform by three wooden steps, rounded a microscopic gravel path, and he unlocked the door of his carriage. It was still faintly marked FIRST CLASS, but it also bore a crusted brass plate whose shining rilievo announced THE VILLA ROSE. He bowed me inwards, invited me to take a pew (his word for an upholstered carriage seat), filled my billy-can from a white enamelled bucket ('Pure spring water!') and, to expedite matters further, insisted on boiling it for me on his Primus stove. As we waited, he sat opposite me. We both looked out the window at the marshes. I heard a Guard's whistle and felt our carriage jolt away to nowhere. We introduced ourselves.

'I trust you find my beach a pleasant spot for a picnic?' he said, as if he owned the entire Irish Sea.

I told him that I had come here about six times over the past thirty years.

'I came here three years ago. When I retired.'

I asked about his three winters. His fingers dismissed them. 'Our glorious summers amply recompense.' At which exact moment I heard sea birds dancing on the roof and Mr Bodkin became distressed. His summer and his beach were misbehaving. He declared that the shower would soon pass. I must have my cup of afternoon tea with him, right there. 'In first-class comfort.' I demurred; he insisted. I protested gratefully; he persisted tetchily. I let him have his way, and that was how I formed Mr Bodkin's acquaintance.

It never became any more. I saw him only once again, for five minutes, six weeks later. But, helped by a hint or two from elsewhere – the man who kept the roadside shop at the end of the lane, a gossipy barmaid in the nearest hamlet – it was enough to let me infer, guess at, induce his life. Its fascination was that he had never had any. By comparison, his beach and its slight sand dunes beside the railway track were crowded with incident, as he presently demonstrated by producing the big album of pressed flowers that he had been collecting over the past three years. His little ear finger stirred them gently on their white pages: milfoil, yarrow, thrift, sea daisies, clover, shepherd's-needle, shepherd's-purse, yellow bedstraw, stone bedstraw, great bedstraw, Our-Lady's-bedstraw, minute sand roses, different types of lousewort. In the pauses between their naming, the leaves were turned as quietly as the wavelets on the beach.

One December day in 1912, when he was fifteen, Mr Bodkin told me, he had entered his lifelong profession by becoming the messenger boy in Tyrrell's Travel Agency, located at 15 Grafton Street, Dublin. He went into Dublin every morning on the Howth tram, halting it outside the small pink house called The Villa Rose, where he lived with his mother, his father, his two young sisters and his two aunts . . .

The Villa Rose! He made a deprecatory gesture – it had been his mother's idea. The plays and novels of Mr A. E. Mason were popular around 1910. He wrinkled his rosy nose. It was not even what you could call a real house. Just two fishermen's cottages joined front to back, with a dip, or valley, between their adjoining roofs. But what a situation! On fine days, he could see, across the high tide of the bay, gulls blowing about like paper, clouds reflected in the still water, an occasional funnel moving slowly in or out of the city behind the long line of the North Wall; and away beyond it, all the silent drums of the Wicklow Mountains. Except on damp days, of course. The windows of The Villa Rose were always sea-dimmed on damp days. His mother suffered from chronic arthritis. His father's chest was always wheezing. His sisters' noses were always running. His aunts spent half their days in bed.

'I have never in my life had a day's illness! Apart from chilblains. I expect to live to be ninety.'

The great thing, it appeared, about Tyrrell's Travel Agency was that you always knew where you were. The Tyrrell system was of the simplest: Everybody was addressed according to his rank. (Mr Bodkin did not seem to realize that this system was, in his boyhood as in mine, universal in every corner of the British Empire.) Whenever old Mr Bob wanted him, he shouted 'Tommy!' at the top of his voice. After shouting at him like that for about five years, Mr Bob suddenly put him behind the counter, addressed him politely as 'Bodkin' and shouted at him no longer. Five years passed and, again without any preliminaries, Mr Bob presented him with a desk of his own in a corner of the office and addressed him as 'Mr Bodkin.' At which everybody in the place smiled, nodded or winked his congratulations. He had arrived at the top of his genealogical tree. He might fall from it. He would never float beyond it. Very satisfactory. One has to have one's station in life. Yes?

The summer shower stopped, but not Mr Bodkin. (In the past three years, I wondered if he had had a single visitor to talk to.) There were, I must understand, certain seeming contradictions in the system. An eager ear and a bit of experience soon solved them all. For example, there was the case of old Clancy, the ex-Enniskillener Dragoon, who opened the office in the morning and polished the Egyptian floor tiles. Anybody who wanted him always shouted, 'Jimmy!' Clear as daylight. But whenever old Lady Kilfeather came sweeping into the agency from her grey Jaguar, ruffling scent, chiffon, feather boas and Protestant tracts, she clancied the whole bang lot of them.

'Morning, Tyrrell! Hello, Bodkin! I hope Murphy has that nice little jaunt to Cannes all sewn up for myself and Kilfeather? Clancy, kindly read this leaflet on Mariolatry and do, for heaven's sake, stop saying "Mother of God!" every time you see me!'

The aristocratic privilege. The stars to their stations; the planets in their stately cycles about the sun; until the lower orders bitch it all up. Meaning old Mrs Clancy, swaying into the office like an inebriated camel, to beg a few bob from Clancy for what she genteelly called her shopping. Never once had that woman, as she might reasonably have done, asked for 'Jim.' Never for 'Mr Clancy.' Never even for 'my husband.' Always for 'Clancy.' Mr Bodkin confessed that he sometimes felt so infuriated with her that he would have to slip around the corner to the Three Feathers, to calm his gut with a Guinness and be reassured by the barman's 'The usual Mr B.?' Not that he had ever been entirely happy about that same B. He always counted it with a stiff, 'Thank you, Mr Buckley.'

It was the only pub he ever visited. And never for more than one glass of plain. Occasionally, he used to go to the theatre. But only for Shakespeare. Or Gilbert and Sullivan. Only for the classics. Opera? Never! For a time, he had been amused by Shaw. But he soon discarded him as a typical Dublin jackeen mocking his betters. Every Sunday, he went to church to pray for the king. He was nineteen when the Rebellion broke out. He refused to believe in it. Or that the dreadful shootings and killings of the subsequent Troubles could possibly produce any change. And did they? Not a damned thing! Oh, some client might give his name in the so-called Irish language. Mr Bodkin simply wrote down, 'Mr Irish.' Queenstown became Cobh. What nonsense! Kingstown became Dun Laoghaire. Pfoo! Pillar boxes were painted green. The police were called Guards. The army's khaki was dyed green. All the whole damned thing boiled down to was that a bit of the House of Commons was moved from London to Dublin.

Until the Second World War broke out. Travel stopped dead. The young fellows in the office joined the army. He remembered how old Mr Bob – they ran the office between them – kept wondering for weeks how the Serbians would behave this time. And what on earth had happened to those gallant little Montenegrins? When the Germans invaded Russia, Mr Bob said that the Czar would soon put a stop to that nonsense. Mind you, they had to keep on their toes after 1945. He would never forget the first time a client said he wanted to visit Yugoslavia. He took off his glasses, wiped them carefully, and produced a map. And, by heavens there it was!

There had been other changes. His mother had died when he was forty-three. His two aunts went when he was in his fifties. To his astonishment, both his sisters married. His father was the last to go, at the age of eighty-one. He went on living, alone, in The Villa Rose, daily mustering thousands of eager travellers around Europe by luxury liners, crowded packet boats, Blue Trains, Orient Expresses, Settebellos, Rheingolds, alphabetical-mathematical planes. He had cars waiting for some, arranged hotels for others, confided to a chosen few the best places (according to 'my old friend Lady Kilfeather') to dine, drink and dance, and he never went anywhere himself.

'You mean you *never* wanted to travel?'

'At first, yes. When I could not afford it. Later, I was saving up for my retirement. Besides, in my last ten years there, the whole business began to bore me.'

He paused, frowned and corrected himself. It had not 'begun' to bore. His interest in it had died suddenly. It happened one morning when he was turning back into the office after conducting Lady Kilfeather out to her grey Jaguar. Observing him, young Mr James had beckoned him into his sanctum.

'A word in your ivory ear, Mr Bodkin? I notice that you have been bestowing quite an amount of attention on Lady Kilfeather.'

'Yes, indeed, Mr James! And I may say that she has just told me that she is most pleased with us.'

'As she might well be! Considering that it takes six letters and eight months to get a penny out of the old bitch. That woman, Mr Bodkin, is known all over Dublin as a first-class scrounger, time waster and bloodsucker. I would be obliged if you would in future bear in mind three rather harsh facts of life that my aged parent seems never to have explained to you. Time is money. Your time is my money. And no client's money is worth more to me than any other client's money. Take it to heart, Mr Bodkin. Thank you. That will be all for now.'

Mr Bodkin took it to heart so well that from that morning on, all those eager travellers came to mean no more to him than a trainload of tourists to a railway porter after he has banged the last door and turned away through the steam of the departing engine for a quick smoke before the next bunch arrived.

Still, duty was duty. And he had his plans. He hung on until he was sixty-five and then he resigned. Mr James, with, I could imagine, an immense sense of relief, handed him a bonus of fifty pounds – a quid for every year of his service, but no pension – shook his hand and told him to go off to Cannes and live there in sin for a week with a cabaret dancer. Mr Bodkin said that for years he had been dreaming of doing exactly that with Mrs Clancy, accepted the fifty quid, said a warm goodbye to everybody in the office, sold The Villa Rose and bought the tarred railway carriage at Cobbler's Hulk. He had had his eye on it for the past five years.

The night he arrived at Cobbler's Hulk, it was dry and cold. He was sweating from lugging two suitcases down the dark lane. The rest of his worldly belongings stood waiting for him in a packing case on the grass-grown platform. For an hour, he sat in his carriage by candlelight, in his blue chesterfield, supping blissfully on the wavelets scraping the shingle every twenty seconds and on certain mysterious noises from the wildlife on the marshes. A snipe? A grebe? A masked badger?

He rose at last, made himself another supper of fried salty bacon and two fried eggs, unwrapped his country bread and butter and boiled himself a brew of tea so strong that his spoon could almost have stood up in it. When he had washed his ware and made his bed, he went out on to his platform to find the sky riveted with stars. Far out to sea, the light of a fishing smack. Beyond them, he thought he detected a faint blink. Not surely, a lighthouse on the Welsh coast? Then, up to the line, he heard the hum of the approaching train. Two such trains, he had foreknown, would roar past Cobbler's Hulk every twenty-four hours. Its headlamps grew larger and brighter and then, with a roar, its carriage windows went flickering past him. He could see only half a dozen passengers in it. When it died away down the line, he addressed the stars.

'O Spirits, merciful and good! I know that our inheritance is held in store for us by Time. I know there is a sea of Time to rise one day, before which all who wrong us or oppress us will be swept away like leaves. I see it on the flow! I know that we must trust and hope, and neither doubt ourselves nor doubt the good in one another ... O Spirits, merciful and good, I am grateful!'

'That's rather fine. Where did you get that?'

'Dickens. *The Chimes.* I say that prayer every night after supper and a last stroll up the lane.'

'Say it for me again.'

As he repeated those splendid radical words, he looked about as wild as a grasshopper. 'Thinner than Tithonus before he faded into air.'

Had he really felt oppressed? Or wronged? Could it be that, during his three years of solitude, he had been thinking that this world would be a much nicer place if people did not go around shouting at one another or declaring to other people that time is money? Or wondering why Mother should have had to suffer shame and pain for years, while dreadful old women like Kilfeather went on scrounging, wheedling, bloodsucking, eating and drinking their way around this travelled world of which all he had ever seen was that dubious wink across the night sea? He may have meant that in his youth, he had dreamed of marriage. He may have meant nothing at all.

He leaned forward.

'Are you sure you won't have another cup of tea? Now that I can have afternoon tea any day I like, I can make a ridiculous confession to you. For fifty years, I used to see Mr Bob or Mr James walk across Grafton Street every day at four-thirty precisely to have afternoon tea in Mitchell's Café. And I cannot tell you how bitterly I used to envy them. Wasn't that silly of me?'

'But, surely, one of the girls on the staff could have brewed you all a cup of tea in the office?'

He stared at me.

'But that's not the same thing as afternoon tea in Mitchell's! White tablecloths? Carpets? Silverware? Waitresses in blue and white?'

We looked at each other silently. I looked at my watch and said that I must get going.

He laughed happily.

'The day I came here, do you know what I did with *my* watch? I pawned it for the sum of two pounds. I have never retrieved it. And I never will. I live by the sun and stars.'

'You are never lonely?'

'I am used to living alone.'

'You sleep well?'

'Like a dog. And dream like one. Mostly of the old Villa Rose. And my poor, dear mamma. How could I be lonely? I have my beautiful memories, my happy dreams and my good friends.'

'I envy you profoundly,' I said.

On which pleasant lying coda we parted. For is it possible never to be lonely? Do beautiful memories encourage us to withdraw from the world? Not even youth can live on dreams.

He had, however, one friend.

One Saturday evening in September, on returning from the wayside shop on the carriage road, he was arrested by a freshly painted sign on a gate about two hundred yards from the railway track. It said FRESH EGGS FOR SALE. He knew that there was not a house nor a human being in sight. Who on earth would want to walk a mile down this tunnelled lane to buy eggs? Behind the wooden gate, there was a grassy track, leading, he now presumed, to some distant cottage invisible from the lane. He entered the field and was surprised to see, behind the high hedge, an open shed sheltering a red van bearing, in large white letters:

FLANNERY'S
HEAVENLY BREAD

After a winding quarter of a mile, he came on a small, sunken, freshly whitewashed cottage and knocked. The door was opened by a woman of about thirty-five or forty, midway between plain and good-looking, red-cheeked, buxom, blue-eyed, eagerly welcoming. She spoke with a slight English accent that at once reminded him of his mother's voice. Yes! She had lovely fresh eggs. How many did he want? A dozen? With pleasure! Behind her, a dark, heavily built man, of about the same age, rose from his chair beside the open turf fire of the kitchen and silently offered him a seat while 'Mary' was getting the eggs.

Mr Bodkin expected to stay three minutes. He stayed an hour. They were the Condors: Mary, her brother Colm – the dark, silent man – and their bedridden mother lying in the room off the kitchen, her door always open, so that she could not only converse through it but hear all the comforting little noises and movements of her familiar kitchen. Their father, a herdsman, had died three months before. Mary had come back from service in London to look after her mother, and poor Colm (her adjective) had come home with her to support them both. He had just got a job as a roundsman for a bakery in Wicklow, driving all day around the countryside in the red van.

Mr Bodkin felt so much at ease with Mary Condor that he was soon calling on her every evening after supper, to sit by the old woman's bed, to gossip or to read her the day's news from his *Irish Times* or to give her a quiet game of draughts. That Christmas Day, on Mary's insistence, he joined them for supper. He brought a box of chocolates for Mary and her mother, one hundred cigarettes for Colm and a bottle of grocer's sherry for them all. He recited one of his favourite party pieces from Dickens. Colm so far unbent as to tell him about the bitter Christmas he had spent in Italy with the Eighth Army near a place called Castel di Sangro. Mary talked with big eyes of the awful traffic of London. The old woman, made tipsy by the sherry, shouted from her room about the wicked sea crossing her husband had made during 'the other war,' in December of 1915, with a herd of cattle for the port of Liverpool.

'All travelled people!' Mr Bodkin laughed, and was delighted when Mary said that, thanks be to God, their travelling days were done.

As he walked away from their farewells, the channel of light from their open door showed that the grass was laced with snow. It clung to the edges of his carriage windows as he lay in bed. It gagged the wavelets. He could imagine it falling and melting into the sea. As he clutched the blue hot water bottle that Mary had given him for a Christmas present, he realized that she was the only woman friend he had made in his whole life. He felt so choked with gratitude that he fell asleep without thanking his spirits, the merciful and the good, for their latest gift.

What follows is four fifths inference and one fifth imagination; both, as the event showed, essentially true.

On the Monday of the last week in July, on returning from the roadside shop with a net bag containing *The Irish Times*, tea, onions and a bar of yellow soap, Mr Bodkin was startled to see a white Jaguar parked beside the level crossing. It was what they would have called in the travel agency a posh car. It bore three plaques, a GB, a CD and a blue-and-white silver RAC. Great Britain. *Corps Diplomatique*. Royal Automobile Club. He walked on to his platform to scan the beach for its owner. He found her seated on his bench, in a miniskirt, knees crossed, wearing a loose suède jacket, smoking a cigarette from a long ivory holder, glaring at the grey sea, tiny, blonde (or was she bleached?), exquisitely made up, still handsome. Her tide on the turn. Say, fifty? He approached her as guardedly as if she were a

83

rabbit. A woven gold bangle hung heavily from the corrugated white glove on her wrist. Or was it her bare wrist? Say, fifty-five? Her cigarette was scented.

'Fog coming up,' he murmured politely when he came abreast of her and gave her his little bobbing bow. 'I do hope you are not waiting for a train.'

She slowly raised her tinted eyelids.

'I was waiting for you, Mr Bodkin,' she smiled. (One of the sharp ones?)

Her teeth were the tiniest and whitest he had ever seen. She could have worn them around her neck. Last month, he saw a field mouse with teeth as tiny as hers, bared in death.

'Won't you sit down? I know all about you from Molly Condor.'

'What a splendid woman she is!' he said and warily sat beside her, placing his net bag on the bench beside her scarlet beach bag. He touched it. 'You have been swimming?'

'I swim,' she laughed, 'like a stone. While I waited for you, I was sun-bathing.' She smiled for him. 'In the nude.'

Hastily, he said, 'Your car is *corps diplomatique*!'

'It is my husband's car. Sir Hilary Dobson. I stole it!' She gurgled what ruder chaps in the agency used to call the Gorgon Gurgle. 'You mustn't take me seriously, Mr Bodkin. I'm Scottish. Hilary says I am fey. He is in the F. O. He's gone off on some hush-hush business to Athens for a fortnight, so I borrowed the Jag. Now, if it had been Turkey! But perhaps you don't like Turkey, either? Or do you? Athens is such a crumby dump, don't you agree?'

'I have never travelled, Lady Dobson.'

'But Molly says you once owned a travel agency!'

'She exaggerates my abilities. I was a humble clerk.'

'Eoh?' Her tone changed, her voice became brisk. 'Look, Bodkin, I wanted to ask you something very important. How well do you know Molly Condor?'

He increased his politeness.

'I have had the great pleasure of knowing Miss Mary Condor since last September.'

'I have known her since she was twenty-two. I trained her.

She was in my service for twelve years. But I have never looked at Molly as just a lady's maid. Molly is my best friend in the whole world. She is a great loss to me. Of course, as we grow older, the fewer, and the more precious, our friends become.'

He considered the name, Molly. He felt it was patronizing. He had never lost a friend – never, before Mary, having had one to lose. He said as much.

'Too bad! Well! I want Molly to come back to us. My nerves have not been the same since she left.'

He looked silently out to sea. He was aware that she was slowly turning her head to look at him. Like a field mouse? He felt a creeping sensation of fear. Her nerves seemed all right to him. He watched her eject her cigarette, produce another from a silver case, insert it, light it smartly with a gold lighter and blow out a narrow jet of smoke.

'And then there is her brother. Condor was our chauffeur for five years. It would be simply wonderful if they both came back to us! I know poor old Hilary is as lost without his Condor as I am without my Molly. It would be a great act of kindness if you could say a word in our favour in that quarter. Hilary would appreciate it no end. Oh, I know, of course, about the mother. But that old girl can't need the two of them, can she? Besides, when I saw her this morning, I had the feeling she won't last long. Arthritis? *And* bronchitis? *And* this climate? I had an old aunt just like her in Bexhill-on-Sea. One day, she was in splendid health, The next day, her tubes were wheezing like bagpipes. For six months, I watched her, fading like a sunset. In the seventh month . . .'

As she wheedled on and on, her voice reminded him of a spoon inside a saucepan. He listened to her coldly, with his eyes, rather than his ears, as for so many years he used to listen to old ladies who did not know where exactly they wanted to go nor what they wanted to do, alert only to their shifting lids, their mousy fingers, their bewildered shoulders, their jerking lips. Crepe on her neck. French cigarettes. Sun-bathing nude. Bodkin. Condor. Molly. 'Poor old Hilary.' What did this old girl really want? Coming all this way for a lady's maid? My foot!

'And you know, Bodkin, Molly has a great regard for you.

She thinks you are the most marvellous thing she ever met. I can see why.' She laid her hand on his sleeve. 'You have a kind heart. You will help me, if you can, won't you?' She jumped up. 'That is all I wanted to say. Now you must show me your wonderful *wagon-lit*. Molly says it is absolutely fab.'

'I shall be delighted, Lady Dobson,' he said and, unwillingly, led her to it.

When she saw the brass plate of THE VILLA ROSE, she guffawed and hastened to admire everything else. Her eyes trotted all over his possessions like two hunting mice. She gushed over his 'clever little arrangements.' She lifted potlids, felt the springiness of the bed, penetrated to his water closet, which she flushed, greatly to his annoyance because he never used it except when the marshes were very wet or very cold, and then he had to refill the cistern with a bucket every time he flushed it.

'I find it all most amusing, Bodkin,' she assured him as she powdered her face before his shaving mirror. 'If you were a young man, it would make a wonderful weekend love nest, wouldn't it? I must fly. It's nearly lunchtime. And you want to make whatever it is you propose to make with your soap, tea and onions. Won't you see me to my car? And do say a word for me to Molly! If you ever want to find me, I'm staying in the little old hotel down the road. For a week.' She laughed naughtily. 'Laying siege! Do drop in there any afternoon at six o'clock for an aperitif,' and she showed half her white thigh as she looped into her car, started the engine, meshed the gears, beamed at him with all her teeth, cried, '*A bientôt*, Bodkin,' and shot recklessly up the lane, defoliating the hedges into a wake of leaves like a speedboat.

Watching her cloud of dust, he remembered something. A chap in the office showing him a postcard of *Mona Lisa*. 'Ever seen her before? Not half! And never one of them under fifty-five!' Indeed! *And* indeed! 'I am afraid, Lady Dobson, we must make up our minds. A cool fortnight in Brittany? Or five lovely hot days in Monte Carlo? Of course, you *might* win a pot of money in Monte Carlo . . .' How greedily their alligator eyelids used to blink at that one! He returned slowly to his *wagon-lit*, slammed down the windows to let out the smell of her cigarette, washed the dust of yellow powder from his washbasin, refilled his cistern and sat for an hour on the edge of his bed, pondering. By nightfall, he was so bewildered that he had to call on Mary.

She was alone. The old lady was asleep in her room. They sat on either side of the kitchen table, whispering about the hens, the up train that had been three minutes late, the down train last night that was right on the dot, the fog that morning, both of them at their usual friendly ease until he spoke about his visitor. When he finished, she glanced at the open door of the bedroom.

'I must say, she was always very generous to me. Sir Hilary was very kind. He went hard on me to stay. He said, "You are good for her." She had her moods and tenses. I felt awfully sorry for him. He spoiled her.'

'Well of course, Mary, those titled people,' Mr Bodkin fished cunningly and was filled with admiration for her when she refused to bite.

All she said was, 'Sir Hilary was a real gentleman.'

'They are married a long time?'

'Fifteen years. She is his second wife. She nursed his first wife. But I *had* to come back, Mr Bodkin!'

'You did quite right. And your brother did the right thing, too. I mean, two women in a remote cottage. Your brother is never lonely?'

She covered her face with her hands and he knew that she was crying into them.

'He is dying of the lonesome.'

From the room, the old woman suddenly hammered the floor with her stick.

'Is he back?' she called out fretfully.

Mary went to the bedroom door and leaned against the jamb. It was like listening to a telephone call.

'It's Mr Bodkin . . . He went up to the shop for cigarettes . . . I suppose he forgot them . . . About an hour ago . . . He may be gone for a stroll. It's such a fine night . . . Och, he must be sick of that old van . . .' She turned her head. 'Was the van in the shed, Mr Bodkin?' He shook his head. 'He took the van . . . For God's sake, Mother, stop worrying and go to sleep. He maybe took the notion to drive over to Ashford for a drink and a chat. It's dull for him here . . . I'll give you a game of draughts.'

Mr Bodkin left her.

A nurse? It was dark in the lane, but above the tunnel of the hedges, there was still a flavour of salvaged daylight. He started to walk towards the road, hoping to meet Condor on his way back. The air was heavy with heliotrope and meadowsweet. A rustle in the ditch beside him. Far away, a horse whinnied. He must be turned forty by now. Behind him, Africa, Italy, London. Before him, nothing but the road and fields of his boyhood. Every night, that solitary cottage. The swell of the night express made him look back until its last lights had flickered past the end of the lane and its humming died down the line.

But I have lived. An old man, now, twice a child.

By the last of the afterlight above the trees of the carriage road, he saw the red nose of the van protruding from the halfmoon entrance to the abandoned manor house. He walked to it, peered into its empty cabin, heard a pigeon throating from a clump of trees behind the chained gates. He walked past it to the shop. It was closed and dark. He guessed at a lighted window at the rear of it, shining out over the stumps of decapitated cabbages. Condor was probably in there, gossiping. He was about to turn back when he saw about one hundred yards farther on, the red taillights of a parked car. Any other night, he might have given it no more than an incurious glance. The darkness, the silence, the turmoil of his thoughts finally drew him warily towards it along the grassy verge. Within fifteen yards of it, he recognized the white Jaguar, saw the rear door open, the inner light fall on the two figures clambering out of it. Standing on the road, they embraced in a seething kiss. When he released her, she got into the driver's seat, the two doors banged and everything was silent and dark again. She started her engine, floodlit the road and drove swiftly away around the curve. Crushed back into the hedge, he heard Condor's footsteps approach, pass and recede. In a few moments, the van's door banged tinnily, its headlamps flowered, whirled into the maw of the lane, waddled drunkenly behind the hedges, down towards the sea.

Before he fell asleep that night, Mr Bodkin heard a thousand wavelets scrape the shingles, as, during his long life, other countless waves had scraped elsewhere unheard – sounds, moments, places, people to whose lives he had never given a thought. *The Irish Times* rarely recorded such storms of passion and, when it did, they broke and died far away, like the fables that Shakespeare concocted for his entertainment in the theatre. But he knew the Condors. This adulterous woman could shatter their lives as surely as he knew, when he opened his eyes to the sea sun shimmering on his ceiling, she had already shattered his.

It was his custom, on such summer mornings, to rise, strip off his pyjamas, pull on a bathing slip and walk across the track in his slippers, his towel around his neck, down to the edge of the sea for what he called a dip: which meant that since he, too, swam like a stone, he would advance into the sea up to his knees, sprinkle his shoulders, and then, burring happily at the cold sting of it, race back to the prickly gravel to towel his shivering bones. He did it this morning with the eyes of a saint wakened from dreams of sin.

On Tuesday night, he snooped virtuously up the lane and along the carriage road. The red van was not in its shed. But neither was it on the road. Lascivious imaginings kept him awake for hours. He longed for the thunderbolt of God.

On Wednesday night, it was, at first, the same story; but on arriving back at the foot of the lane, there were the empty van and the empty Jaguar before him, flank to flank at the level crossing. He retired at once to his bench, peering up and down the beach, listening for the sound of their crunching feet, determined to wait for them all night, if necessary. Somewhere, that woman was lying locked in his arms. The bared thigh. The wrinkled arms. The crepey neck.

Daylight had waned around nine o'clock, but it was still bright enough for him to have seen shadows against the glister of the water, if there had been shadows to see. He saw nothing. He heard nothing but the waves. It must have been nearly two hours later when he heard their cars starting. By the time he had flitted down to the end of the platform, her lights were already rolling up the lane and his were turning in through his gateway.

Mr Bodkin was at the gate barely in time to see his outline dark against the bars of the western sky. As he looked at the van, empty in its shed, it occurred to him that this was one way in which he could frighten him – a warning message left on the seat of the van. But it was also a way in which they could communicate with each other. Her message for him. His answer left early in the morning at her hotel.

On Thursday night, the van lay in its shed. But where was Condor? He walked up the grass track to the cottage and laid his ear to the door. He heard Mary's voice, his angry voice, the mother's shouting. He breathed happily and returned to his bed.

On Friday morning, the Jaguar stood outside Mary's wooden gate. Laying siege? That night, the scarlet van again lay idle in its pen. Wearied by so much walking and watching, he fell asleep over his supper. He was awakened around eleven o'clock by the sound of a car. Scrambling to his door, he was in time to see her wheeling lights hit the sky. He went up the lane to the van, looked around, heard nothing, shone his torch into the cabin and saw the blue envelope lying on the seat. He ripped it open and read it by torchlight. 'Oh, My Darling, for God's sake, where are you? Last night and tonight, I waited and waited. What has happened? You promised! I have only one more night. You are coming back with me, aren't you? If I do not see you tomorrow night, I will throw myself into the sea. I adore you, Connie.' Mr Bodkin took the letter down to the sea, tore it into tiny pieces and, with his arms wide, scattered them over the receding waves.

That Saturday afternoon, on returning from the shop with his weekend purchases in his net bag, there was the Jaguar beside the level crossing, mud-spattered and dusty, its white flanks scarred by the whipping brambles. Rounding the corner of the waiting-room, he saw her on his bench, smoking, glaring at the sparkling sea. She barely lifted her eyes to him. She looked every year of sixty. He bowed and sat on the bench. She smelled of whiskey.

'What an exquisite afternoon we are having, Lady Dobson. May I rest my poor bones for a moment? That lane of mine gets longer and longer every day. Has everything been well with you?'

'Quite well, Bodkin, thank you.'

'And, if I may ask, I should be interested to know, you have, I trust, made some progress in your quest?'

'I could hardly expect to with that old woman around everybody's neck. I have laid the seeds of the idea. Molly now knows that she will always be welcome in my house.'

'Wait and see? My favourite motto. Never say die. Colours nailed to the mast. No surrender. It means, I hope, that you are not going to leave us soon.'

'I leave tonight.'

'I do hope the hotel has not been uncomfortable.'

'It is entirely comfortable. It is full of spinsters. They give me the creeps.'

He beamed at the sea and waited.

'Bodkin! There is one person I have not yet seen. For Hilary's sake, I ought to have a word with Condor. Have you seen him around?'

Her voice had begun to crumble. Eyes like grease under hot water. Cigarette trembling.

'Let me think,' he pondered. 'On Thursday? Yes. And again last night. We both played draughts with his mother. He seemed his usual cheerful self.'

She ejected her cigarette and ground it into the dust under her foot.

'Bodkin! Will you, for Christ's sake, tell me what do young people do with their lives in Godforsaken places like this? That lane must be pitch dark by four o'clock in the winter!'

He looked at his toes, drew his handkerchief from his breast pocket and flicked away their dust.

'I am afraid, Lady Dobson, I no longer meet any young people. And, after all, Condor is not a young man. I suppose you could call him a middle-aged man. Or would you?'

She hooted hoarsely.

'And what does that leave me? An old hag?'

'Or me? As the Good Book says, "The days of our years are threescore years and ten; and if by reason of strength they be fourscore years, yet is their strength labour and sorrow; for it is soon cut off, and we fly away." '

She spat it at him:

'You make me sick.'

From under her blue eyelids, she looked at the clouds crimped along the knife of the horizon. He remembered Mary's twisted face when she said, 'He is dying of the lonesome.' She turned and faced him. Harp strings under her chin. Hands mottled. The creature was as old as sin.

'Do you happen to know, Bodkin, if Condor has a girl in these parts? It concerns me, of course, only in so far as, if he has, I need not ask him to come back to us. Has he?'

Mr Bodkin searched the sea as if looking for a small boat in which to escape his conscience.

'I believe he has,' he said firmly.

'Believe? Do you know? Or do you not know?'

'I saw them twice in the lane. Kissing. I presume that means that they are in love.'

'Thank you, Bodkin,' she said brightly. 'In that case, Hilary must get another chauffeur and I must get another lady's maid.' She jumped up. He rose politely. 'I hope you all have a very pleasant winter.' She stared at him hatefully. 'In love! Have you ever in your life been in love? Do you know what it means to be in love?'

'Life has denied me many things, Lady Dobson.'

'Do you have such a thing as a drink in that black coffin of yours?'

'Alas! Only tea. I am a poor man, Lady Dobson. I read in the paper recently that whiskey is now as much as six shillings a glass.'

Her closed eyes riveted her to her age like a worn face on an old coin.

'No love. No drink. No friends. No wife. No children. Happy man! Nothing to betray you.'

She turned and left him..

The events of that Saturday night and Sunday morning became public property at the inquest.

Sergeant Delahunty gave formal evidence of the finding of the body on the rocks at Greystones. Guard Sinnott corroborated. Mr T. J. Bodkin was then called. He stated that he was a retired businessman residing in a chalet beside the disused station of Cobbler's Hulk. He deposed that, as usual, he went to bed on the night in question around ten o'clock and fell asleep. Being subject to arthritis, he slept badly. Around one o'clock, something woke him.

CORONER: What woke you? Did you hear a noise?
WITNESS: I am often awakened by arthritic pains in my legs.
CORONER: Are you quite sure it was not earlier than one o'clock? The reason I ask is because we know that the deceased's watch stopped at a quarter to twelve.
WITNESS: I looked at my watch. It was five minutes past one.

Continuing his evidence, the witness said that the night being warm and dry, he rose, put on his dressing gown and his slippers and walked up and down on the platform to ease his pains. From where he stood, he observed a white car parked in the lane. He went towards it. He recognized it as the property of Lady Constance Dobson, whom he had met earlier in the week. There was nobody in the car. Asked by a juror if he had seen the car earlier in the night, before he went to bed, the witness said that it was never his practice to emerge from his chalet after his supper. Asked by another juror if he was not surprised to find an empty car there at one o'clock at night, he said he was but thought that it might have run out of petrol and been abandoned by Lady Dobson until the morning. It did not arouse his curiosity. He was not a curious man by nature. The witness deposed that he then returned to his chalet and slept until six o'clock, when he rose, rather earlier than usual, and went for his usual morning swim. On the way to the beach, he again examined the car.

CORONER: It was daylight by then?
WITNESS: Yes, sir.
CORONER: Did you look inside the car?
WITNESS: Yes, sir. I discovered that the door was unlocked and I opened it. I saw a lady's handbag on the front seat and a leather suitcase on the rear seat. I saw that the ignition key was in posi-

tion. I turned it, found the starter and the engine responded at once. At that stage, I became seriously worried.

CORONER: What did you do?

WITNESS: I went for my swim. It was too early to do anything else.

Mr Bodkin further stated that he then returned to his chalet, dressed, shaved, prepared his breakfast and ate it. At seven o'clock, he walked to the house of his nearest neighbours, the Condors, and aroused them. Mr Colm Condor at once accompanied him back to the car. They examined it and, on Mr Condor's suggestion, they both drove in Mr Condor's van to report the incident to the Guards at Ashford.

CORONER: We have had the Guards' evidence. And that is all you know about the matter?

WITNESS: Yes, sir.

CORONER: You mean, of course, until the body was found fully clothed, on the rocks at Greystones a week later; that is to say, yesterday morning, when, with Sir Hilary Dobson and Miss Mary Condor, you helped identify the remains?

WITNESS: Yes, sir.

CORONER: Did you have any difficulty in doing so?

WITNESS: I had some difficulty.

CORONER: But you were satisfied that it was the body of Lady Constance Dobson and no other.

WITNESS: I was satisfied. I also recognized the woven gold bangle she had worn the day I saw her. The teeth were unmistakable.

Dr Edward Halpin of the sanatorium at Newcastle having given his opinion that death was caused by asphyxiation through drowning, the jury, in accordance with the medical evidence, returned a verdict of suicide while of unsound mind. The coroner said it was a most distressing case, extended his sympathy to Sir Hilary Dobson and said no blame attached to anybody.

It was September before I again met Mr Bodkin. A day of infinite whiteness. The waves falling heavily. Chilly. It would probably be my last swim of the year. Seeing him on his bench – chesterfield, bowler hat, grey spats, rolled umbrella (he would need it from now on), his bulging net bag between his feet, his head bent to one side as if he were listening for a train – I again wondered at a couple of odd things he had said at the inquest; such as his reply to a juror that he never emerged from his railway carriage after supper; his answer to the coroner that he was often awakened at night by his arthritis ('I sleep like a dog,' he had told me. 'I have never in my life had a day's illness, apart from chilblains'); and he had observed by his watch that it was five past one in the morning ('I live by the sun and the stars'). Also, he had said that from the platform, he had noticed the white car parked at the end of the lane. I had parked my Morris a few moments before at the end of the lane and, as I looked back towards it now, it was masked by the signal box.

He did not invite me to sit down and I did not. We spoke of the sunless day. He smiled when I looked at the sky and said, 'Your watch is clouded over.' I sympathized with him over his recent painful experience.

'Ah, yes!' he agreed. 'It was most distressing. Even if she was a foolish poor soul. Flighty, too. Not quite out of the top drawer. That may have had something to do with it. A bit spoiled, I mean. The sort of woman, as my dear mother used to say, who would upset a barrack of soldiers.'

'Why on earth do you suppose she did it? But I shouldn't ask; I am sure you want to forget the whole thing.'

'It is all over now. The wheel turns. All things return to the sea. She was crossed in love.'

I stared at him.

'Some man in London?'

He hesitated, looked at me shiftily, slowly shook his head and turned his eyes along his shoulder towards the fields.

'But nothing was said about this at the inquest! Did other people know about it? Did the Condors know about it?'

His hands moved on his umbrella handle.

'In quiet places like this, they would notice a leaf falling. But where so little happens every secret becomes a buried treasure that nobody mentions. Even though every daisy on the dunes knows all about it. This very morning, when I called on Mary Condor, a hen passed her door. She said, "That hen is laying

out. Its feet are clean. It has been walking through grass." They
know everything. I sometimes think,' he said peevishly, 'that
they know what I ate for breakfast.'

(Was he becoming disillusioned about his quiet beach?)

'How did you know about it? Or are you just guessing?'

He frowned. He shuffled for the second time. His shoulders
straightened. He almost preened himself.

'I have my own powers of observation! I can keep my eyes
open, too, you know! Sometimes I see things nobody else sees. I
can show you something nobody else has ever seen.'

Watching me watch him, he slowly drew out his pocketbook
and let it fall open on a large visiting card. I stooped forward to
read the name. LADY CONSTANCE DOBSON. His little finger
turned it on to its back. There, scrawled apparently in red lip-
stick, was the word *Judas*. When I looked at him, he was smiling
triumphantly.

'Where on earth did you find it?'

'That morning at six o'clock, it was daylight. I saw it stuck
inside the windscreen wipers' – he hesitated for the last time –
'of the Jaguar.'

My mind became as tumbled as a jigsaw. He was lying. How
many other pieces of the jigsaw were missing? Who was it said
the last missing bit of every jigsaw is God?

'You did not mention this at the inquest.'

'Should I have? The thought occurred to me. I decided that it
would be more merciful not to. There were other people to
think of. Sir Hilary, for one. And others.' He replaced his
pocketbook and rose dismissively. 'I perceive that you are going
for a swim. Be careful. There are currents. The beach shelves
rapidly. Three yards out and the gravel slides from under your
feet. And nobody to hear you if you shout for help. I had my
usual little dip this morning. Such calm. Such utter silence. The
water was very cold.'

He bobbed and walked away. I walked very slowly down to
the edge of the beach. I tested the water with my hand. He was
right. I looked around me. I might have been marooned on
some Baltic reef hung between an infinity of clouds and a lustre
of sea gleaming with their iceberg reflections. Not a fishing

smack. Not even a cormorant. Not a soul for miles, north and south. Nobody along the railway track. Or was somebody, as he had suggested, always watching?

If he were concealing something, why had he admitted that he had come out from his railway carriage at all? Why did he choose to mention one o'clock in the morning? Did he know that she had died around midnight? Was he afraid that some-body besides himself might have seen her lights turn down the lane? A timid liar, offering a half-truth to conceal the whole truth?

Above the dunes, I could just see the black roof of his rail-way carriage. I measured the distance from where I stood and let out a loud 'Help!' For ten seconds, nothing happened. Then his small, dark figure rose furtively behind the dunes. When he saw me, he disappeared.

Foreign Affairs

Georgie Freddy Ernie Bertie Atkinson's mature speech style when holding forth at the bar of the Hibernian United Services Club went something like this – though he would doubtless dismiss it complacently as a vulgar parody of an inimitable original; a pastiche, or, if he were in his Italian vein *un pasticcio*, or in his French mood *un pastichage*, or in his Old French humour a *pasté* ('As the Old French used to say'), or if in a Latin frame of mind a *pasta* ('As Cicero might have said'), or if in his Greek role a $\pi\delta\sigma\tau\dot{\eta}$.

'Hear *my* case!' he might orotundate to the bar. 'When I, at the tender age of approximately twenty minutes and an unspecified number of seconds, at or around ten in the morning on November 11th, 1918, was tenderly deposited in my father's outstretched and trembling arms by the woman who had for so long borne me, none other, I am relieved to be able to say, than his dear wife Eliza, it is not surprising, in view of the day and the hour, forever after to be remembered as Armistice Day, that the bloody old fool should have instantaneously decided to christen me George Frederick Ernest Albert, to express his fervent gratitude, not to the Lord God, in which case he might prophetically have christened me Lord Atkinson, but to King George the Fifth, Reigning Majesty of the United Kingdom of Great Britain and Ireland, head of the once more triumphant Empire, as well as of a whole lot of other institutions ranging from titular admiral of the Royal Fleet to Colonel of the Canadian Mounties, titles and subtitles all, as anyone may absorb in a twenty-five minutes' perusal of any half-decent British almanack spelled with a K.

'Now, when I say that my dear fathead of a father decided thus to label me for life I do not wish to suggest that he calmly made up his mind to do so, and that having made it up he did so. In my experience my father was as nearly mindless as it is possible for any man to be while engaged in selling insurance policies with, it would appear, unusual success, to the normally improvident Irish. I merely wish to convey that he did what he did as absently as one winds one's watch at midnight after heaving one's beloved to the other side of the bed to unwind herself as best she can. Yet, I do assure you gentlemen that, even after I discovered to my cost what exactly he had done to me, I could not find it in my heart to blame him for his folly, nor – and here I do raise my index finger in solemn oath – can I fault him for it even now.

'After all, in that far-off Dublin of 1918 how much common sense could one reasonably expect from a man of his class, origins, upbringing and religious beliefs? Royalist to his rappers, bourgeois to his boots, primitive Methodist Connexion, spelled if you please with an X. Open-air revivalist meetings. Second cousins to the Salvation Army. Hymns in the street under black bowler hats. Belting the Bible like a drum. Come to Jesus! Total certainty of one's own salvation and an even more serene certainty of the damnation of everybody else. How could any such man have foreseen all the political upheavals that within two brief years would turn this British Isle of his fathers' adoption into a free, roaring Irish Republic? Nevertheless, though I forgive the old boy for not having been able to foresee all this political faldirara when he tied "Georgie Freddy Ernie Bertie" to my tail like a firecracker I do blame him, and most severely blame him for having been so unobservant of the meaning and trend of everything happening under his eyes in the years after as to have gone on bestowing on his next four unfortunate children, all distaff, the names of four further members of the English Royal Family. The result is that my eldest sister is now Alexandra Caroline Marie Charlotte Louise Julie. We used to call the second, in my boyhood, Amelia Adelaide and All That Stuff. The third we knew as C.A.I., meaning Caroline Amelia Inc. He christened his fourth and last after that unfortunate bitch Queen Marie Charlotte Sophia of Mecklenburg-Strelitz who was obliged to present her husband

King George III with fifteen brats before, as we all know, his imperial Anglo-Teutonic Majesty went completely off his chump.

'I do not know what agonies my sisters may have had to endure at the hands, or tongues, of their school friends because of those outrageous prefixes. I vividly recall the taunting tones in which, even at school, my more nationalistic fellow Mount-joyians used to hail me as loudly as possible with a "Hello, Georgie Freddy Ernie Bertie," accompanied, when affected by the current xenophobia, by a blaze of homicidal scorn in their green Irish eyes or, if a little less categorically patriotic, the clearest flicker on their lips of what I can only describe as *l'équivoque sympathique* . . .'

A monologuist? That was his form, all right! So infectious that one wants to describe it as port winy, portentous, pompous, pomaded. Any other P's? Patchouli? Well, it is, he was, he *is* an Edwardian hangover. Nevertheless, give the man his due. If he had not had an unfortunate knack of delivering his monologues with such a hang-jawed pelican smile, an archness perilously close to the music hall leer, wink, nudge, lifted eyebrow, he might have ranked with the best of Dublin's legendary monologuists. He lacked their professional self-assurance. However carefully guffers like Wilde, Shaw, Stephens, Yeats or Gogarty prepared their *dits* they always threw them away, assured that there would be an infielder to catch them, an audience to applaud. With Georgie Freddy you were aware of a touch of insecure self-mockery, as if he were always trying to kick his own backside before somebody else did it for him.

'Basta!'

It was his common finale when he wished to indicate that he had made a good point with unusual felicity. Enough on this theme, anyway, to establish that his father was not only a fool but an insuppressible outsider, unusually lucky to have escaped a tarring and feathering, if not assassination, during the revolutionary troubles of the Twenties. And he went on inviting slaughter for years after by bragging every single working day of the year about Georgie Freddy to his eyes-up-to-the-ceiling colleagues during their regular lunch in the crowded basement of Bewley's Oriental Café in Grafton Street. The location is relevant: that it was a café, not a club or restaurant, gives the modest measure of the old chap's commercial standing. Still, though paternal boasting can be boring it can also be touching – one man's daydream is another man's despair. His bored colleagues, remembering their own sons, could sadly shrug. Unfortunately the most aggravating side of the old man's bragging was that Georgie Freddy's career really was outstandingly brilliant from the day he entered Trinity College, Dublin, as a poor sizar to the day he left it with a first class degree in classics, a gold medal in Greek, a sound command of modern Italian and French language and literature, and a good reading knowledge of German. Even more aggravatingly, his career went on being brilliant after he exchanged the university for the British Army in 1942, starting as a lieutenant, promoted to staff-captain in the desert, finally elevated to major in Italy.

With Italy old Bob Atkinson elevated himself to the rank of God the Father. He was now able, thanks to Georgie's dispatches, to gas the whole lunch table of insurance men with prolonged, detailed, hour by hour, beach by beach, blow by blow accounts of how Georgie landed in Sicily at the head of the Eighth Army, advanced to Catania and Messina and crossed between Scylla and Charybdis to the Italian mainland. There, surpassing all, an event occurred that sent the old man into a blazing, vertical takeoff from Bewley's perfumed basement up through every floor and out through the slates of the roof into Dublin's sea-gulled September air.

This event was Georgie's personal encounter with General Alexander, the commander of the Eighth Army, in a war-battered Calabrian hamlet called Galiana at one o'clock of a warm, sticky morning in September shortly after the capture of the city of Reggio di Calabria.

'Think of it, gentlemen!' the old buffer embraces the coffee table with a gleeful laugh. 'There is our brave bucko, Captain George Frederick Ernest Albert Atkinson, my son, my very own son, lying flat on his ass on the upstairs floor of a fleabitten hut in the volcanic mountains of Calabria, dead to God and the

101

world, sound asleep, white as a statue from the dust, and the dirt and the brunt of the battle, shagged from fighting the Eyties the whole bloody sweating day, when he is suddenly shaken awake by one of his fellow officers and a blaze of light blinding his eyes through the windows. He thinks it's the rising sun. It is the headlamps of a military jeep.

' "What in the hell's blazes," says he, "is up now?"

' "Up," sez the officer. "Did you say *up?* You'll soon know what's up," sez he, "if you're not down in five seconds," sez he, "because it's the general that's up," sez he, "that is to say down them ladders thirsting for your blue Oirish blud."

' "What flaming general, for God's sake?" sez our young hero, still lost in the arms of Murphy.

'His comrade stands to attention and sings out the answer as if he was on a barrack square.

' "I refer to General Harold Rupert Leofric George Alexander Irish Guards Military Cross Companion of the Order of the Star of Indiar ADC to His Majesty whom God preserve since 1936 born in Tyrone in good ould Oireland . . ."

'Well, I needn't tell ye, gentlemen, that at the mention of the general's name it didn't take Georgie boy a week of Sundays to get down that ladder, buttoning his uniform. He clatters into the kitchen, salutes to attention, wondering what in God's name Alexander can have let go wrong with the campaign while he was catching a wink of sleep, and gets the usual polite lift of the finger in return.

' "Captain Atkinson," says Alex very quietly, for he is on all occasions most polite and courteous, one of nature's gentlemen, one of the real old Irish stock. "I regret to have to tell you, Captain, that to my nostrils this village stinks. From the point of view of the health and morale of my troops, such dirt is not a good thing. Can you, as the officer in charge of the area, explain to me why it is so?"

'Gentlemen! Does Georgie tremble? Does Georgie blench? Is Georgie rattled? No, gentlemen. Georgie stares Alex straight in the eye, as cool as that cucumber sandwich there on me plate. "Dirty?" sez he, and now don't let us forget that Georgie was a gold medalist in Ancient Greek when he was at Trinity College,

Dublin. "I entirely agree with you, sir. This village stinks to high heaven. It is an absolutely filthy hole. But, sir, if you would care to recall from your days at Eton your Herodotus, book three, chapter four, paragraph one, I think you will remember, sir, that this village has been dirty, evil-smelling and nauseating since the year 434 B.C." Well, gentlemen, do you know what Alex did, at three minutes past one o'clock in the morning in that battered ould canteen in Calabria? He laffed. And he laffed. And he laffed! "I perceive, Captain," he decides at last, "that you are a linguist and a scholar. What other languages do you command besides Greek?" Georgie replies that as well as being a gold medalist in Ancient Greek he speaks fluent Italian, fluent French and has a useful knowledge of German. The general raises the one finger. "The very man for me! Consider yourself promoted from this moment to the rank of major. Report to me at Field H.Q. this morning at seven, ready to assume the post of Military Commander of the city of Reggio di Calabria until further orders." And with that he turns on the leather heel of his brown, polished high boots, climbs into his jeep, leaving Major Atkinson stunned – stunned, gentlemen – as he watches its lights vanishing like a kangaroo into the blackness of the Eyetalian night. And that is how my boy became a major, in command of the first city in Italy taken by Allied troops. Is that, gentlemen, or is that not an astonishing ringside view of contemporary history?'

Undeniably! The coffee cups toast him. If true! The cups are sipped silently. But . . .

Now, we Irish, like certain other peoples honed hard by history – some of them our best friends – are a double helix of softness and hardness, of passion and calculation, which is why one of the men at that table, an envious, nosy, aquiline character named Cooney got so fed up to his zinc-filled molars (insurance salesmen cannot afford gold) with this oft-repeated yarn about Alex and Georgie that he snuck off to consult a professorial friend in the clerical College of Maynooth, who in turn snuck off to an Irish Catholic archaeologist friend in the Dublin Institute for Advanced Studies, about this Methodist yarn about a Calabrian village called Galiana said to have been unflatteringly mentioned by the great Herodotus in the fifth century B.C. After prolonged searching through the entire corpus of the historian's works none of the three of them could find any mention whatever of any such settlement in any known part of Magna Graecia.

Cooney – for even the most cooneyish Cooney in the world has a heart – was far too kind to mention this fact to old Bob Atkinson. Instead, he waited for four years, and for the appropriate jovial company, to tax the then retired major with his lie. The answer he got made him blush slowly from his neck to his chin, to his eyes, to the peak of the rampant cupola of his bald skull.

'There is, of course,' Georgie declaimed, *ore rotundo* as always, 'no mention of any such place in Herodotus. Indeed, only an illiterate would expect to find it there. I simply embellished a trivial but actual encounter to give a little harmless pleasure to an old man, who, by the way, if, sir, the matter is of any interest to you, we moved late last night into Sir Patrick Dun's Hospital, situated beside the canal once justifiably acclaimed as The Grand Canal. It now barely moves. Weedy. Muddy. Tin cans. Dead cats. He moves not at all. His doctor tells me he has not the strength left to die. He will probably float away, like Joyce's last Liffey leaf, to join his cold, old, dreary fathers tonight.'

'You told a lie,' Cooney insisted coldly.

'Mr Cooney, I did speak to General Alexander. I was promoted major. I was O.C. in Reggio di Calabria. And that is not a world away from the ruins of Thurii, on the Italian Ionian, which Herodotus helped to found, and from which, by then a great and famous city, as famous at least as Dublin, he is believed to have finally floated into his own history. May I, Mister Cooney, give my father your kind wishes, whether false or true, before he in his turn returns to his proper sea?'

'Having told one lie,' Cooney said, 'I am sure you can manage another.'

'I admit,' Georgie replied ever so gently, 'that I did allow my imagination a little latitude. It is a national failing. You, unfortunately, do not appear to suffer from it.'

2

Ex-major. Home to roost. Portly. Savile Row suit, blue and grey pinstripe, blue weskit, mother-of-pearl buttons, T.C.D. tie, rolled gamp, *Times*, of London not Dublin, flat folded under right oxter, pallid blue Peep O'Day handkerchief in breast pocket, Italian shoes. At thirty a man with a past, to be taken seriously, for the moment, another wandering fighter returned reluctantly to stay-at-home Dublin. War-scarred by a bullet that grazed his inside right thigh at Potenza. ('Another inch and I'd be a *castrato*.') Far travelled, through France as a beggarly student, through Greece as a frayed-at-the-cuffs classicist, sweating under North Africa's steely sun, Sicily baked him, Magna Graecia rained on him, England demobbed him, Ireland reopened her arms to him. Pensionless.

'My *epikedeion*,' he liked to sigh and to translate. 'My threnody. My graveside oration.'

He was already inventing his own legend to fortify himself, an alien in a city that had been his ever since he burst upon it on that historic morning thirty years ago via Saint Assam's Nursing Home off Hatch Row, in Ballsbridge.

The place is relevant: the prelude to his myth, his *domus omnium venerum*, to be flourished with bravura on all suitable occasions as Dublin's most famous house of pleasure, patronized by procreative jockeys, trainers, handicappers, bloodstock exporters, breeders (also of horses), dignitaries of the Turf Club, pouring in at all hours of the day and night to view the offspring of their loins, as laden with flowers as if Ireland were Hawaii; wine merchants' messenger boys constantly bearing cases of champagne in and out of the wrong bedrooms; lean, goitre-eyed greyhounds lolloping up and down deeply upholstered, much urinated on stairs; a home less given to displaying umbrellas in its hall stands than bridles, hunting crops, horse blinkers as rigid as leather bras. The city of his pimpled and impoverished schoolboy years under the switch of Parson Magee in Mountjoy Square. He recalls the ribald smiles of his bare-kneed fellows whenever they mentioned the double meaning name of a square whose latter-day decline from Georgian *piazza* to Joyceian slum both betrayed and confirmed (pure and total legend this) his ruttish teens. His personal city, his *dolce domum* from the day it flowered superbly, generously, uberto-sely (he invented the word) as a metropolis of the mind during his student days in its major university, founded by Elizabeth the First. The scene and source of his proudest achievements, his *alma noverca* whose knighting queen had transformed (first battering break) this poorborn Methody into newborn gentle-man, man of the world, soldier of the Empire, inheritor of all the ages of the world . . .

'Behold me now!' he loved to groan. 'Back in Ithaca, father-less, motherless, wifeless, loveless, homeless. Our old family home in Mount Pleasant Square sold! O God!' At this his voice would break. 'With the military barracks to the west of us, bugle-calling at dawn, and the monastery to our east, hymning hymns, and the road through Windy Arbour, Dundrum, Sandy-ford, Golden Ball, to the lovely, lonely moors beyond the Scalp; and the canal floating seaward silently past its Dic-kensian tenements on Charlemont Place, every bum painter's delight; and Harcourt Terrace around the corner, odorous of Saint John's Wood, frankincense, classic grace and decadent nineteenth-century vice!

'And now? Not a relative left. My four sad sisters scattered through the British Isles, nursing, typing, clerking, married or otherwise gone to the bitches. As witness my dearest, youngest sister Charlie, she homonymously of Mecklenburg-Strelitz, obliged to marry at seventeen, when apparently – the adverb sounds aerie but is accurate – pregnant by a hot theological student at Trinity. Thereafter obliged, like her famous eponym, to bear his reverence one infant per annum, a fair excome on a poor investment, exiled in a sea-sprayed parsonage on the coast of West Cork, facetiously called "a living," endlessly fertile because, again apparently, neither of them can think of any-thing better to do when the paraffin ebbs in the pink glass bowl of the lamp, and the hearth goes grey and the Atlantic waves claw at the naked shingles of the western world.'

Such groans were masochist – apart from that sincere refer-ence to Mount Pleasant Square. Names like that fell on the ears of his generation like far-off music, the horns of elfland; especially so for every boy come up from the provinces to a Dublin that had been a promise and a legend. For these, now grown men, Dundrum, Windy Arbour, Sandyford, Golden Ball would always happily evoke days of idleness and pleasure in the mountains with their lost girls and their faded youth. They fell like a knell on the memory of the ex-major; he had been too poor, pressed, and pimply for girl-play. Those nostalgic place-names suggested to him the youth he had never had.

Nevertheless! No regrets! Chin up! He was a man! He had campaigned! He had travelled and proved himself! He dismissed his non-youth without an audible sigh, and smartly unpacked his *elegantissimi* bags, purchased in vanquished Rome, in the bedroom of a modest Leeson Street guest house, called *The Anchor*, directly opposite the nuns' hospital, and from this base began thoughtlessly, blissfully, improvidently to live the life of a clubman. The United Services, five minutes across the Green, ten if he dawdled to watch the geese, ducks, seagulls. Its paths were, in the summer, lined with deck chairs, female legs to glance at covertly, an extra paper to buy, a sixpence for the old woman with the flowers outside the Saint Stephen's Green Club who always flattered him with her, 'Ah! God be good to you, *Colonel*!'

At lunch, at the Round Table, there was always somebody to talk to. He could easily kill time after it in the reading room, if lucky in the billiard room, then over afternoon tea in town. He lived extravagantly – his well-earned due – even slipped in a couple of expensive visits to Paris and Cannes. Before the year was out he had the beginnings of a duck's belly. For ten months he flourished. Then, suddenly, always an ominous word, while still abed one damp March morning he found on his breakfast tray, beside his London *Times*, three envelopes that caused his pleasant life to stammer, hiccough, wobble, shake and halt like a car out of petrol. His monthly bank sheet drew his eye swiftly to a total in red.

'Aha!' he laughed. '*Enfin, je suis dans le rouge.*'

The secretary of his Club also politely requested £50 in renewal of his annual subscription, plus £75. 6. 10 for drink and food consumed on the premises during the previous quarter. ('And well worth it!') His London tailor's bill brought him to the ground.

He steadily perused his *Times*, lit a cigarette and gazed calculatingly across the street at the nuns' hospital. Long before he was halfway through his cigarette he agreed that he possessed only one solid asset. His scholarship was unsaleable. Nobody except headmasters of schools would want his gift of languages. Majors were as little in demand in the Dublin of 1949 as Jesuits in the Geneva of 1549. His one solid asset was Moll Wall. He sent her an invitation to dinner at his Club. She agreed happily. With her usual shrewdness she had been expecting it for months.

3

Moll Wall was an Irish-speaking, Dublin-born Jewess whose father was known all over the world to every serious collector of Irish glass and silver. He ran a small antique business on one of the Dublin quays, a widower, the doyen of his profession, respected as a man of knowledge and probity. Alas for his only child, he took so much delight in his craft that he never had time to make money out of it. Accordingly Moll had had to work her way into college by winning scholarships, and knew that when she finished she would always, like her father, be comparatively poor. She worked now in the Department of External Affairs.

At Trinity she had been Georgie Atkinson's only female friend. He had been happy to spend months of hours with her over morning coffees or cups of afternoon tea in cheap cafés – he could never afford to take her to lunch – exchanging carefully prepolished student repartees and epigrams, solemnly discussing politics and languages, especially ancient tongues. They used to talk most warmly about loyalties, which at that time chiefly meant family loyalties and college personalities; spreading out later to international personalities; which in turn gradually hardened into political principles. They talked of religion, especially of its history. Here she had the edge on him, a Jewish mind ranging aeons behind Christianity into the vast Asiatic

desert between the world-mothering rivers, finding everything
he associated with the nineteenth century already matured four
thousand years before in the thoughts of Ur and Babylon. He
never dared to discuss love with her – How could he? He so
poor, she so proper – though she did attract him: lean, hard,
lank, black, bony, muscular – they first met at the Foils Club.
She was his senior, due to leave college before him, stern of
character, good humoured, but also unpredictably puritanical,
a woman whose moral force he frankly feared, whose Jewish
sense of what is righteous and just he burningly admired, whose
chosen vocation he wished he had dared to imitate. But even at
college he was already (that English Connexion) hearing not the
far-off echoes of Babylon but the imminent bellowings of
Hitler, reading Houston Stewart Chamberlain, wondering how
'his' Empire and 'her' race would fare in the years before them.

Her real name was not Moll. It was Miriam, but since in her ex-
cessive efforts to nationalize herself she always signed her name
not only in Gaelic but in an outmoded script, 𝑀𝑎𝑖𝑟𝑒 𝑑𝑒 𝑏𝑎𝑙𝑙 ·
her fellow students called her Moira, or Maurya, or Maureen,
until she ended up by being universally known as Moll Wall.
Whenever she lapsed into one of her more solemn moods they
called her The Wailing Wall. He always respectfully called her
Miriam. She always kindly called him George.

As he watched her sip her abstemious aperitif ('A small dry
sherry, please') he guessed at her age. Thirty-five? Halfway to
three score and ten. Perhaps more? Why had she never married? Took love too solemnly? Warned chaps off? She had
always warned him off. Or was it he who warned her off? No
beauty, yet she did unarguably have her fine points, even if each
of them suffered a 'but' from the poor company it kept. Her
skin was delicate, but tinged like a quarter gypsy's; her black
hair was rich, oily and luxuriant, but it hung straight as threads
beside her fine eyes; which were as lightly blue as two morning
glories but set in eyelids as misshapen as scalene triangles re-
cumbent against the bridge of her Hebraic nose; her teeth were
as healthy and white as the teeth of a hound, but the canines
and incisors crossed voraciously; her lips, if set in a gentler face,
might have been prettily described as bee-stung, but in her

strong countenance their pouting suggested not an insatiable kisser but an insuppressible talker. He liked her best when she laughed with a zany triumph that lit up her whole being. He had seen it often behind the flashing foils. She was at her best there – breastless, black from masked face to hissing foot, strong-calved, aggressively competitive, swift as her mind that was as sharp as a pitiless diamond in the hand of a glasscutter. How often had he not seen her at a public debate in college slash through some speaker's clever sophistry with one clean, arrogant stroke and casually chuck his bits into the rubbish bin beside her. He feared her – she was female. She envied him – he was male.

'You look very well,' he quizzed, raising his glass to her. 'How is life in your wicked Quai d'Orsay?'

'In order,' she smiled.

'Meaning in your order. I do congratulate you, Miriam. You always have ordered your life. Unlike those of us who have lived not wisely but too well, you have lived most wisely if not too well.'

'Where did you steal that piece of wit?'

'Othello. But he said "loved." He, too, admired a dark skin.'

'He too?' She smiled crookedly – it was as far as he would ever go. Timid? Shy? Unsexy? Androgynous? Selfish, like all bachelors? Frightened of women, like all Irishmen. But with her racial humility, her Jewish submissiveness – a female Job, *I have said to the worm Thou art my mother and my sister* – she had long since accepted that for him a wife would always be a poor substitute for the cosy filial relationship that always seemed sufficient for so many Irish *goyim* and so many Jewish Jews. And what if *I have* ordered my life? Had I any alternative? And how well I did it! His useless Greek, my useful Semitic languages, Arabic, Hebrew, even that spot of Aramaic, and then modern Irish, and that second degree in political science.

She could read his mind as if she were sitting inside it.

'George! What is the English for *cul-de-sac*?'

'Blind alley?' he suggested.

Years before he went marching off down his blind alley to the sound of guns and drums, and drums and guns, in defence of an

Empire that even one of his father's actuaries could have told him would be stone dead within ten years, I was within steps of the top in External Affairs. I'd be an ambassador now if I were a man. Some woman once said of penis-envy, 'Who wants the stupid thing anyway?' O God! It must be worth five thousand pounds a year at least. Certainly worth an ambassadorship.

As if he could read her thoughts he told her sympathetically that with her Talmudic mind, so regulative, so legalistic, she was far too honest for foreign service, and, of course, far too idealistic, too romantic, much too sentimental. She hooted with laughter, well used to male romantics boasting of their realism. Ireland is full of them. She calmly declared her role – the *Eminence rose* of Ireland, guiding it knowledgeably through all its conflicts with the wicked world; at which they laughed so merrily that they ended by casting flickering glances of mistrust at one another. It was how they always sparred, advancing, receding to and from some sort of understanding, affinity, or intimacy that seemed to be regarded as best left undefined. One of their comrades once summed it up with, 'They are completely different and they are two of a kind.' And had she not once told him, with the air of somebody passing on a clue in a game, the sad story of the Egyptologist who, on finding a tiny flower in a freshly opened tomb, scooped it out of the dusk, into the sun, where it straightway died.

'I see you have settled back into Dublin all right,' she stated so firmly that he frowned. Had the witch been bugging him for the last ten months?

'I am back,' he shivered at her, 'in the cold bosom of Mother Ireland. Surrogate paps.'

She raised an eyebrow, observed that he had been drinking a lot of wine. On top of three martinis. Lacking courage? To pop his question? Whose nature she foresaw from his joke, disconnected, about owing a debt to his tailor and to society. Through the smoke of his cigar, over his port, her brandy, he finally posed the problem with a blend of bluster and nonchalance, so transparent that her heart was touched. Poor kid! Up against it?

'Miriam, I've come to the end of this bloody city. If you were me what would you do to keep boredom profitably at bay?'

'Join the army.'

'They sacked me a year ago!'

'The Irish army.'

'My God!' he cried rudely. 'A joke army! They are about as martial as the Pope's Swiss Guards. They haven't fought since 1922.'

'Snob. And ignoramus! It is for its size as good an army as any in the world. It also happens that the Swiss Guards have in their time fought skilfully and died bravely. Anyway,' glancing at his midriff, 'most of your fighting was conducted in an office. I must fix you up with some fencing soon. Think about it, George. Good quarters, a good mess – those we have inherited from your British Army – good pay, no expenses, all your financial troubles solved. Okay?'

'Well,' he mumbled, abashed by her penetration, 'I know my merits. I am quite sure I could teach those chaps a thing or two. But what about my deplorable genealogy? Even my name marks me as what your race would call "a gentile."'

'If you have the luck to be even so much as considered by them at all it will be solely because of your deplorably Saxon background. Consider! Our army is aggressively patriotic, ninety-five per cent Roman Catholic, one hundred per cent proletarian. Can't you see the kick we would get out of introducing you with deadpan faces to some visiting foreign brass? "Our Captain Atkinson." The brass looks at you superciliously. You turn out to be a first class Greek Scholar, from a sixteenth-century university, a practising Methodist, ex-British Army, widely travelled, an Oxford accent, commanding five languages. You would be our prize exhibit. Our Uncle Tom.'

His cheeks blazed. She raised two palms and pouted at him with her shoulders, chin, eyebrows, lower lip, even with that shrugging of the bottom known as the *cul de poule*.

'It's what I am, George. Their Auntie Tom. It does not prevent me from doing my job as well as anybody in the department, indeed a hell of a sight better.'

For a while he was too aghast to speak. Finally:

'I am *not*,' he insisted, 'a practising Methodist. And I do *not* speak five languages. I speak only Greek, French, Italian and English.'

She laid her hand on his wrist. His throat gobbled. He looked in astonishment at her radiant eyes and triumphant mouth. She could be damned attractive sometimes.

'The fifth language is the quintessence of our plot. It will be our master stroke. You must also be able to talk Gaelic to visiting brass. In fact I wonder could we put you into kilts?'

'Me?' he railed in his most haughtily offensive tone – excusable, she felt, in a man whom she had been deliberately kicking in the balls. 'I don't know a word of your bloody lingo.'

'My lingo,' she yielded gently, 'is Hebrew. You are a good linguist, George. Almost as good as I am. In six weeks I can teach you enough Irish to get you through the interview. With the strings I can pull for you they will see that you are on a plate for them. After that, the more you behave like a bally ass the more they will love you. But I am afraid you simply must also be some sort of a Protestant because it so happens that by pure luck we just now badly need one to represent the President and the army on such sad occasions as the funerals of such alien sects as Jews, Methodists, Jehovah's Witnesses, Baptists, Orangemen, Free Masons, Buddhists, members of the Church of Ireland and all that pagan lot.'

He gazed at her lean and yellow abstinence. Sardonic bitch! A victim of genes. Also sexual frustration. And a countervailing lust for power. He said grandly that he would 'look them over.' Her sable eyelids drooped. She did not say it but he heard it. 'Good doggy!' Was this the beginning of his servitude or his success?

4

Those army years proved to be the best years of his life. Financed, fed, clothed, housed, flattered, fathered and, he was right, he *could* teach them a thing or two. They asked his views about lots of things – about cigars, wines, cricket, social protocol, Methodism, French letters, the English public school system, cocktails, gloves, ties, polo, English whores, John

Wesley, The Royal Family, London clubs. Splendid fellows. Most intelligent. Some of my best friends.

If only, he sighed sincerely to her – and she smoothly agreed – they had some cultural interests. To remedy this, being unmarried and with no more than a peripheral interest in Woman and none in Marriage he was able to afford a secret, tiny, pink-papered bedsitter in the city where he could store his L.P. records, his beloved Loeb Classics, his French novels, relax in his Hong Kong pyjamas, sip a *pastis*, or a *Punt e Mes*, or a *retsina*, or a *Chambéry vermouth*, or a *cassis vin blanc*, unfold his *Times*, smoke a ten-shilling cigar, even entertain a rare female acquaintance. Naturally he never told Moll about this hideaway. She would have closed her bistre eyelids and laughed with her blue serpentine tongue at his rosy refuge. She would have known at once that he would have lost more battles there with Dublin's virgins than would bankrupt the honour of an entire army in any other part of the globe except Uganda, Israel and Maoist China. She was pleased that he did, now and again, take her to dinner at his Club. There he always had the grace to thank her for what she had done for him. Secretly he wished she had less moral character and more immoral flesh.

Those lovely fat years ended the day he heard her, to his bewilderment, abruptly telling him on the telephone that he was wasting his talents in the army and that he must stop it at once. He invited her to dinner in the Club. There she repeated her extraordinary opinion. He bluntly told her to mind her own damned business, he was hunkydory where he was, he had every intention of going on being hunkydory, and thank her VERY much! He saw her lower lip curl. He saw her slanted canines. He also noted, with an ingenuous satisfaction, that she seemed to have no ready reply – she merely changed the subject. That, he decided, was the way to do it. Treat them rough. A month later he discovered from a chummy note slipped under his door that he was about to be transferred to a civilian post in the Department of Defence. He at once sent her a dispatch, by motor cyclist, marked *Supremely Urgent*, informing her that as soon as he had put his affairs in order he would resign. The final haughty sentence of this dispatch recalled

Alfred de Musset. *On ne badine pas avec moi!* Unfortunately a month of frantic search showed him that Fate *could* trifle with him. She had rightly assumed penury, hoped for boredom, was satisfied that he would not succeed in locating any alternative income. She had experienced it all herself.

He suffered in the Department of Defence. Why had he ever been so foolish as to return home to this mist-shotten island? If only, he groaned, there were another war, another lovely, bloody, muddy, dusty, murderous war to free him from this womb! Nevertheless, as a man of courage, an Odysseus, he must suffer Ithaca! And Penelope! He gave up his London *Times*. He had to surrender his pink-papered hideaway, sell his Loebs, wear cotton pyjamas, even have his suits off the rack. But he clung, by God, he clung to his Club. *On ne badine pas* ... It should be the motto of the arms of the Atkinsons. He endured his lot until, perceptibly, some secret powers realized his true worth. He gradually found himself being used as a liaison between External Affairs and Defence, involving certain (not always intelligible, but nonetheless always welcome) explorations of the continent of Europe, for four weeks at a time and not less than four times a year. Bit by bit his bitter blood became sweeter, until, on a day no different to any other, he decided now that he had taught the foolish woman a lesson – namely that his worth would always be appreciated by somebody – he could afford to be generous. He took her back into his favour. He invited her to dinner at his Club.

5

Before the night was out she realized sadly that the Civil Service had taught him only a little. She knew his age to the hour, as who did not, forty-two on November 11th. He was as portentous as if he were still twenty-seven, a trifle less supercilious, capable at last of an occasional two minutes' silence. He found her as alert as always, regrettably one of those women who bear the lineaments of unsatisfied desire, as garrulous as ever but, now that he had learned what a desk and a dictaphone can do to the human spirit, he had to admire the way she had preserved her identity over the years *senza rancor.* It was the foils, he presumed, that preserved her sanity. No swordsman can feel rancour against an opponent who slips a blade under his defence.

All in all it was a most pleasant evening. Warmed by the wine he was so daring as to say to her as they parted on the pavement outside her flat, 'As Mr Churchill once said to Mr Roosevelt, *Amantium irae amoris integratio est.*' He cautiously spoiled it by adding, 'The maxim is also found in Publilius Cyrus, Maxim twenty-five. Speaking also of the quarrels of lovers as a renewal of friendship's bond.' She was to recall the moment as a missed opportunity. If only she had said – even with so shy a man, so conditioned a Methody, so late in the game – 'Aren't you going to kiss me good night?' she might have saved him some shame and herself some misery. Her excuse could only have been that at that moment she was gazing past him at the lamps of the square like a painter before his landscape, a sculptor before his model, a writer before his theme, wondering what the hell to do next to, with or for so intractable a subject. She merely said, 'Thanks for a delightful dinner, George! Good night!'

Sin loomed. Pride, vainglory, hubris, even some of that very bumptiousness that she held against him. It was natural, to be sure, that she should want not only to have his apple on her tree but to pluck it, feel it in the palm of her hand, under her eye, shining on her own desk, in her own department – she managed it easily even though she was well aware that it is the one department whose men are supposed to be mobile, even nomadic. 'But not our George!' George was no pilot; he was ground staff, a born adjutant, no more. She was amusedly confident of it – until, against her vehement, fervent, pleading, even irascible advice her superiors insisted on posting him as Second Secretary to the Paris embassy. When, in a drawling voice, he told her that, after careful consideration, he had agreed to accept this minor post, she foresaw with satisfaction that within a month Paris would return him to her lap.

To her rage he succeeded brilliantly there. A year later the powers beyond her control (and understanding) decided to send the boy to Oslo. He succeeded there as impeccably. Two years later she shudderingly saw him depart as First Secretary in the embassy to the Quirinal. Within a month he was the toast of Rome's diplomatic corps. (*Questi Irlandesi! Argutissimi! Spiritosi! Un gros gaillard. Ces Irlandais! Jolly able chap, take him for an Englishman any day. Ein so witziger Kerl.*) She gave in. Anyway she knew that the whispering gallery of the department had long since marked him down as their *Eminence rose*'s personal creation. She had no option left but to pilot him to greater and greater achievements. An embassy? But not too far away! Canberra was mentioned. She cursed the Corona Australis in Irish. Africa offered. She Hebrewed it into a fog. Canada produced an obscenity in Arabic. The hand of chance crept forward on two fingers towards the E.E.C. The United States of Europe? *Chef de cabinet* in the Commission for Culture and Civilization? That would be worthy of her. But there was one danger. The U.S.E. is supranational. Its officers serve Europe, not their own country. She could have him sent on a string – seconded. Even so, to recall him might not be easy. Threatened by Australia, Canada and Africa, she yielded.

Brussels. 1972. *And Belgium's capital had gathered then her beauty and her chivalry.* A few miles north of Waterloo. *To arms! And there was mounting in hot haste ... Or whispering with white lips. 'The foe! They come! They come!'*

6

She came one sunny November morning. Her cold camera's eye smilingly interrupts and startlingly arrests one of his slow and stately steps as, bearing his fawn gloves, rolled gamp, bowler hat, he strolls from and now proudly leads her back to his modest but elegant three-roomed apartment on the Avenue des Arts.

'I chose it myself as befitting my not inconsiderable rank in the bureaucratic hierarchy of the new supranational Europe.'

His housekeeper, a lean, dark, sallow Flamande of middle age, makes them some excellent fresh French coffee, and Moll settles back to consider her protégé.

To her knowledge, she informs him, he is now fifty-four.

'Matured and wise?' she hopes.

She is, he flatters her, by his reckoning fifty. 'Would I wish any contemporary older?'

His living-room she finds most untidy: letters, newspapers, books, magazines, reports on this and that all strewn about.

'My fingers itch.'

He is, she mocks, bloated from vanity and luxury. She is, he quips, lean from unsatisfied desire. She retorts with the fat weed that roots itself in ease on Lethe's wharf. He pulls in his gut.

'An elegant suit, it flatters your figure, George.'

'A charming frock. Do I perceive one teeny grey hair? The vanity of that necklet must have set you back at least a hundred pounds.'

Husband and wife could not have sparred more equivocally, each with reason. He would have preferred an ambassadorship and is sure she has denied it to him. He is behaving arrogantly just to show that he has slipped out of my power. He owes her more than his pride approves. She could do so much, oh, so very much more for him if only he would be a tiny bit more accommodating. At which point they both suddenly experienced a painful revelation of shared loss. In small countries like the green island to which they both belonged – as in all small cities, towns, houses, offices, institutions, workshops throughout the world – familiarity breeds envy, and that conspiracy, and that skulduggery – it is their greatest disadvantage. However, just because they are so close, so small, so familiar, so personal, so intimate, one understands their skulduggery – it is one of their greatest advantages. Here? One can never keep track of the conspiracies of impersonal, ever-shifting Babels like the League of Nations, The United Nations, The Council of Europe, the E.E.C. They both suddenly begin to talk about Dublin, its gossip, its personalities, its plotters and planners, its news, its . . . It was she who, in the end, had to rise, and sadly send him about his business. Still, as she went her way she was humming, *He might have been a Rooshian, | A French or Turk or Prooshian | Or perhaps Itali-AN, | But in spite of all temptations | To belong to other nations, | He still remains an Irishman.*

In high good humour she fished among her own informants around the city – the U.S.E. had already brought some four hundred Irish to Brussels – took stock, weighed up, relaxed, expanded and returned to Dublin satisfied at long last with her offspring, her everything, husband, uncle, aunt, father, mother, sister, brother, fat, folly, power, freedom, fame. She began to boast of My Man in Bruxelles. She paced the corridors of power, moved across the chessboard of mirrored Europe, equipped with almost a dozen western and eastern languages, dropping amiably into this office and that, thriving on all those old Dublin yarns, legends, memories, characters, another Irish wit. From that on she flowered in the sun of his delightfully regular, secret dispatches from the front, intimate vignettes, witty, salted by a touch of the malicious, the flirtatious, even the salacious. He revelled in hers, so full of naughty local gossip. For them both it was like being back in T.C.D. all over again, except that she began to dress more and more carefully, had her straight hair waved every week, favoured restaurants where the headwaiter called her Madame, flaunted costume jewellery, wore Chamade scent and, the department groaned, talked like a bloody minister. During the next nine months she visited him there four times and he returned four times to Dublin. It was his heyday, her green period, his mature style period, the time when from Dublin she possessed Europe. A year passed. Never the tiniest spray of yew.

It was around the second quarter of his second year that the dry palmetta leaves of gossip began to clack. Long accustomed to such mutterings she made nothing of them. A woman? She laughed sardonically. The palm leaves still rattled their loose skin in the wind. What woman? She laughed in hysterical relief. She had met the poor creature five times. His hard-working, middle-aged, plain, surly, dark, unprepossessing, skinny house-keeper. Her assurance persisted until the September afternoon when:

Dear Miriam,

I have last week been here for exactly a year and a half, and I can say in all modesty that we have left our mark on Europe. I have now decided to show the flag. Accordingly I have taken a roomy

apartment at 132 *bis*, two blocks farther along the avenue where I
can suitably house a visitor or entertain a colleague. There are three
bedrooms, one for me, one for a guest, one for my housekeeper,
Miss Virginia Nieders. You may remember Ginnie. Or did you even
notice her at all? She is a splendid cook and, as I have just discovered, a superb if expensive shirtmaker, a marvellous find. She is
Flemish and in many ways a remarkable creature. Lean as a grey-
hound, blackhaired, sallow as tallow, a coiled spring of energy, eyes
shadowed as if by a gauze of libidinous soot, filled with a proud,
Aristophanic scorn of all mankind, most entertainingly outspoken
about my international colleagues, and especially about their wives.
Where *does* she collect all this scandal? Moody if reproved, even
thunderous, but absolutely devoted to me. And what a vocabulary!
You would enjoy it. Yesterday evening I said that it was a charming
sunset. She cried, '*C'est transcendant.*' Last week when she was
fitting one of her splendid shirts on me I mentioned to her that it
was rather tight under the armpits. What did this child of nature
reply? She cried out in agony, in Walloon – though she can speak
French too – that her soul was lacerated. Can you imagine any
woman of any other race relating souls and shirts? Except perhaps
an Italian? *Mi straccia l'anima!*' But these Flemish women can be
highly tempestuous creatures. If I did not accept this as a fact of
nature I do not think I could, or even should have put up with some
of her more outspoken remarks about our visitors. Anyway, it is a
charming apartment and the next time you come to Brussels you
must bring a chaperon and stay with us.

Ever, G.

Another woman reading this letter might have merely raised
a speculative eyebrow, wonderingly turned down the corners of
the mouth. Moll, who knew her man to the backbone, not so
much turned the pages as whirled them. At the imprecise word
'our' in 'our visitors' she stopped breathing. At the final sentence she became taut, at the final word 'us' her spring snapped.
'Our' visitors? Her finger accused him. Rage blinded her. The
fool wondered where the woman got her amusing scandals? She
saw one of those inevitable international *kaffee-klatschen* of
valets, hall porters, cooks, maids, chauffeurs, housekeepers, remembered her first glance about his earlier apartment, the
untidy desk, the letters and papers strewn about it, covered her

face in fury at the thought of her letters to him being eagerly deciphered over so many full-breasted and elbowed kitchen tables. She pulled herself up, and back. The essential word was not 'our.' It was the final word 'us.' When he wrote that word he convicted himself.

She must make certain. But could anybody ever know for certain what exactly, if anything, had happened between these two idiots. Not even he, perhaps he least of all, for when men of his age compromise themselves they lose all touch with reality. Her brain went cold and her heart went hard for one concentrated hour by which time she had established five points.

1. Though nothing is impossible in this area, it was unlikely that he had slept with her.

2. Even if he had she was not affected by the slightest feeling of jealousy – on this she had to be clear, and was.

3. Something either had happened, was happening, or was about to happen, well-known to Brussels, as the gossip at home showed, implying enough laughter in the *coulisses,* the *couloirs,* the cafés to show her that he was letting down the side.

4. The crunchy bit. An international U.S.E. aide is beyond the direct control of his home country: unless, *a.,* he has made such a fool of himself as to embarrass his resident Minister or *b.,* deeply offended his own resident racial community (in this case the proper, puritanical, R.C., inferiority-complexed and supersensitive Irish), or, best/worst of all, *c.,* created gross scandal or ribald laughter at home.

5. There was one way in which he just might be persuaded to do Number 4, *c.*

She sat to her typewriter and wrote to him, in French, her thanks for his invitation, and of her joy and delight at all the dear letters he had been sending to her over the last year or so. She had at last broken their secret code, she had lifted the curtain of their timid and, for that very reason, all the more delightful intimations. She understood, at last, all that his dear, fond heart had so tremulously been trying to say. 'How blind I have been! How my heart burns to think of all the days and nights we shall have together!' She would be in his arms in Brussels by next Friday night, happy that they need no longer conceal their passion from the world. Of course, she would be charmed to stay with him, *sans* chaperon. In fact he must send that silly old housekeeper on a holiday for the weekend. *Je me prends a pleurer de joie. Je t'embrasse.* M.

It was Wednesday. She posted her letter, to his new flat, before noon. She left the flap open. He (they) should be reading it by Friday morning. She had left him no time to reply by letter. He would not risk telephoning. The answer must be a telegram, and everything would now depend on its tone. It would be a blisterer if he was completely innocent; a blusterer if he was half innocent; evasive if he were guiltily unsure about whatever the hell he had or had not been up to. If he was guilty he would rush across to Dublin at once to find out what precisely he had been guilty of in his sleep.

His telegram came on Friday afternoon. AM FLYING TO DUBLIN FRIDAY SOONEST WILL TELEPHONE FROM CLUB SATURDAY MORNING SOONEST. EVER, GEORGE.

She no sooner read it than she found herself unable to swallow. Could the idiot – she was prepared to swear in open court that the possibility had not occurred to her before – could he, whether innocent or guilty, have taken her declaration *au pied de la lettre*? She suffered a night of sleeplessness, nightmare and nervous indigestion while pondering on all the uncomfortable as well as on some of the pleasing if also tormenting implications of the idea. He did not telephone on Saturday morning. Instead, the hall porter at his Club did, to tell Miss Miriam Wall that The Major had arrived, after a bad crossing, had a cold and neuralgia, was confined to his room, but would ring her in the afternoon. An hour later a great heap of red roses arrived from the florist near the Club. She extra-mured them in the hall. What was this all about? Oozing courage? For what? Up to some trickery? She waited indoors all day. He did not telephone.

He had decided to let her wait, which is to say that – like his old father long ago who could never make up his mind about anything – he was cowering in his room, not with a bad cold and neuralgia but with a bad conscience and nerves. He had already had a scene with one woman in Brussels; he could not bring himself to face another scene in Dublin. Let her be the one to telephone! Dammit! Was he a man or a mouse? (His honest insides whispered, 'Mouse!') Around five o'clock, being just about to descend to the bar for a bracer, a knock at his door and the page boy outside informed him that a lady of the name of Wall was inquiring for him downstairs.

He had always said it! Treat them rough! He tremblingly brushed back the greying wings of his green fifties, checked the lie of his tie, plucked the dark red handkerchief in his breast pocket an inch higher and then with stately tread slowly descended the winding stairs to meet the wench. There below him, foreshortened in the middle of the tessellated hall, stood Virginia Nieders, black-clothed, blackhaired, her black spring wound tight, the aureoles about her eyes as brown as thunder. Cornered, even a mouse will bare its tiny teeth. Reverting instantly to type Major Atkinson strode past her to the porter's glass box, whipped out his wallet, slipped a fiver into the man's hand, said, 'Get rid of her at once,' emerged, howled at her in Walloon, French, Flemish, English and Italian, 'Go away!', while bounding in long leaps like an obese giraffe for the stairs. Behind him the porter's brass-buttoned tails did such an effective flying tackle about her whirling waist that two arriving diners, both rugby threequarters, cheered his grappling speed. A lifted telephone, a Guard opportunely passing, peacock screams in English, French and Flemish diminuendoed into the street. Calm returned to the Hibernian United Services Club. The porter stood staring at her through the barred glass door. The Guard stood warily watching her from the balcony of the double steps. Georgie leaned from the tiptop bedroom of the club peering at her glistening poll until God sent the miracle of a cloudburst whose downpour washed her ark away.

The Major galloped downstairs, rang for a taxi, drove to his old Guest House on Leeson Street. They were delighted to see him. But there was no room in the inn. Oh! A foreign lady, they slyly said, had been asking after him only an hour ago. Phew! Being without his address book he drove on to External Affairs, on Saint Stephen's Green, to collect a few friendly telephone numbers from the usual solitary Casabianca holding the Saturday fort. He had barely time to shout 'Full speed ahead' to the cabby before she bounded like a dripping mermaid from the portico down to the pavement to shriek in Flemish after him. He remembered an old Irish army friend who had a base on Earlsfort Terrace, around the corner from the Green. Terror poured its adrenaline all over his kidneys at the sight of her black, spearlike figure under the spotlight of that portico too. 'Down the Hatch!' he roared, and with whistling tyres down the Hatch they went. Were there ten of her? He must think. He must have a drink. He must eat. Round the Green to the Unicorn. Or had he by chance spoken to her of that estimable restaurant as a haunt of his legendary student days? He evidently had. Peeping from his knees on the floor of the taxi, he saw her against the restaurant's lighted, curtained window. He surrendered. Back to the Club! There for the first time in his life he was relieved to find the bar empty. It took him half an hour and three brandies to clarify the situation.

What were the simple facts? He shook his head wildly. Damnation! What *were* the simple facts? He had been lonely. Right? She had been lonely. Right? What more natural than that he should want to comfort her, be kind to her? Right? And if he ever had gone beyond that whose business was it but his own? Anyway everybody knew that half the international population of Brussels was living in sin – except the cagy Irish. It would all have been hunkydory if the cow hadn't pulled the teat out of the baby's bottle. Chasing him over here in broad daylight! And God knows what she had been saying to whatever junior she had found across the Green in External Affairs! And, no doubt, she would be back there on Monday morning screaming fit for a French farce. Right? No! Yes!!!

He was a ruined man.

A third brandy was needed to give him the courage to ring for the firing squad.

'Miriam! It is me. I'm simply dying to see you.'

'George!'

She sounded sad. Could she be shy? How dicey was this going to be? He tried to make his own voice sound neither soft nor hard. It came out as hoarse as an old hinge.

'I needn't tell you, Miriam, that I'd have rung you at once if it hadn't been for this wretched cold.'

'Your poor cold! Caught, I presume, racing around Dublin from that woman.'

His stomach fell a foot.

'How soon can I see you, Miriam?'

'I am afraid not tonight, George. Nor tomorrow. Ever since your housekeeper arrived in Dublin she has been telephoning me every half hour. You must have confided greatly in her, she is so accurately informed about this city. Have you been telling her all about your golden youth? Also you left your address book behind you. For all I know she may have rung the Secretary. Even the Minister. Perhaps the entire Cabinet? Some little while ago she took up her position on the pavement opposite my flat, parading up and down under the rain between two lamp-posts like an unemployed whore. After watching her through my curtains for half an hour I brought her in. Soaked to the skin, poor slut! I gave her a stiff drink, let her pour some of her European despair over me, gave her some dry clothes and sent her to soak in a hot bath where she is wallowing at this moment. When she emerges I suppose I shall have to listen to a few more lurid revelations about our man in Bruxelles before I park her in some modest guest house where she can prepare herself for her interview with the Secretary on Monday morning.'

'But the woman is daft, Miriam! You can't, nobody can believe a word she says!'

'It is not only what she says, it is what she sees. She says you have a mole in the small of your back. Have you, George?'

'She makes shirts for me!'

'How intimate! And that you have a scar on the inside of your right thigh.'

'I must have mentioned it to her.'

'She has a letter you wrote to her from Paris two months ago. It almost made me blush.' Her voice became soft and sad again. 'I am sorry, George. You ought to have stayed in Trinity and become a tutor in Ancient Greek. I realize now that what you are is a man so afraid of the lonely, little Irish boy in you that

125

you have grown fold after fold of foreign fat to keep him in
Just as this poor woman may well have had an exuberant Peter
Paul Rubens goddess bursting to get out of her skinny body
ever since the day she was born. O dear! I sometimes wonder
how many Ariels were imprisoned in Caliban. And how many
Calibans were imprisoned in Ariel? It is a thought that makes
one feel sorry for the whole human race.'

'Well!' he blustered, 'since you are so damned sorry for the
whole human race would you kindly tell me what I had best do
now?'

'That is quite simple. You have only two alternatives. The
first is to resign and return. You would have to accept a spot of
demotion. But, never fear, we will find a cosy berth for you
somewhere. A consulate in South America? In Africa? Say in
Uganda? We won't let you starve. The other possibility you
must surely have gathered from my letter. If you should still
wish me to announce that we have been privately engaged for
the past six months you can blow the whole business out like a
candle. But you must decide at once so that I may ring up the
Secretary, or the Minister, and a gossipy friend or two, and
have it published in Monday's *Irish Times*, and break it gently
to the poor slut upstairs, and drive her to the airport tomorrow.
You could then break off our engagement at your convenience.
Only, in that case, George, please do, I beg you, return my
letter. It puts me so completely in your power as a woman.'

She knew that the flattery of that last bit would be irresistible.

'You mean . . . I mean . . . You mean you meant all that in
your letter?'

'George! Do you not realize how attractive you are to
women?'

He answered her without hesitation in the voice of a small
boy saying, 'Mummy! May I go to the pictures?':

'Miriam! Let us be married at once.'

'I hear her bath water running out. At once cannot be too
soon, George. I must hurry. Get on a plane for Brussels *il più
presto*. If you don't she will strip our flat naked and then set fire
to it. Good night, darling. Ring me from Brussels.'

For a long time he looked with a dazed smile into the mouth

126

f the receiver. He carried the same smile to his mirror. At-
ractive to women? Well! He brushed his greying wings,
hucked his lapels, arranged his lolling peony handkerchief,
milingly went downstairs to dinner. What a woman! Such tact,
bility, foresight! He would have ample time for dinner before
atching the last plane for London. His concierge in Brussels
vould do the rest. Touching his empty *boutonnière* at the turn
f the stairs his descent was halted by a memory: her story of
ne rash Egyptologist whose frail flower wilted at the sight of
ay.

She, hit at that precise moment by a memory of a different
ort, hastily concluded a swift good night to her most gossipy
ossip –

'Happy? I remember what happened to poor Pygmalion. He
vorked for years on a statue of the perfect woman and found
imself left with a chatterbox of a wife. I think of all the years I
ave devoted to my chatterbox.' She laughed philosophically.
Never mind. I am really very fond of poor old George. I
lways have been. And he needs me. I must fly. Tell the world!'

As she replaced the receiver she turned in her chair to watch
he china handle of the door slowly turning. When it was
hrown wide open her eyes stared at her dark visitor staring at
er, wearing the long, soft, white, woollen shawl, interwoven
vith gold thread, always kept in tissue in her tallboy, the gold
orque that had so diverted George, three bracelets from her
ressing-table on each scraggy arm, and a red rose in the black
nat of her hair. For one statuesque second the door became a
evelled mirror asking, 'And who is who, now?' Then, reso-
utely conquering her weakness, she rose and advanced with her
rms wide open.

'Virginia!'

They sat side by side on the cosy sofa beside the fire. There,
peaking ever so gently, but firmly, she tenderly, gradually,
lmost absentmindedly, woman to woman, stripped her guest of
er dreams and her plumes. From both a few tears, a shrug, a
ug and, in three or four languages, 'Men!'

Falling Rocks, Narrowing Road, Cul-de-sac, Stop

The day Morgan Myles arrived in L— as the new county librarian he got a painful boil under his tongue. All that week he was too busy settling into his new quarters to do anything about it beyond dribbling over his mother's hand mirror into a mouth as pink and black as a hotel bathroom. Otherwise he kept working off the pain and discomfort of it in outbursts of temper with his assistant, Marianne Simcox, a frail, long-legged, neurotically efficient, gushingly idealistic, ladylike (that is to say, Protestant) young woman whom he hated and bullied from the first moment he met her. This, however, could have been because of his cautious fear of her virginal attractiveness.

On his fourth day in the job he was so rude to her that she turned on him, called him a Catholic cad, and fled sobbing behind the stacks. For fifteen minutes he went about his work humming with satisfaction at having broken her ladylike ways; but when she failed to come trotting to his next roar of command, he went tearing around the stacks in a fury looking for her. He was horrified to find her sitting on the floor of the Arts Section still crying into her mouse-sized handkerchief. With a groan of self-disgust he sat on the floor beside her, put his arm around her shoulder, rocked her as gently as if she was a kid of twelve, told her he was a bastard out of hell, that she was the most efficient assistant he had ever had in his life and that from this time on they would be doing marvellous things together with 'our library.' When she had calmed, she apologized for being so rude, and thanked him so formally, and so courteously, and in such a ladylike accent that he decided that she was a born bitch and went off home in a towering temper to his mother who, seeing the state her dear boy was in, said, 'Wisha, Morgan love, why don't you take that gumboil of yours to a doctor and

128

show it to him. You're not your natural nice self at all. You're as cranky as a bag of cats with it.'

At the word 'doctor' Morgan went pale with fear, bared his teeth like a five-barred gate and snarled that he had no intention of going next nor nigh any doctor in this one-horse town. 'Anyway,' he roared, 'I hate all doctors. Without exception of age or sex. Cods and bluffers they are, the whole lot of them. And you know well that all any doctor ever wants to do with any patient is to take X-rays of his insides, order him into hospital, take the clothes down off of him, stick a syringe into his backside and before the poor fathead knows where he is there'll be half a dozen fellows in white nightshirts sawing away at him like a dead pig. It's just a gumboil. It doesn't bother me one bit. I've had dozens of them in my time. It's merely an Act of God. Like an earthquake, or a crick in the neck. It will pass.'

But it did not pass. It went on burning and smarting until one windy sunstruck afternoon in his second week when he was streeling miserably along the Dublin Road, about a mile beyond the town's last untidy lot, beside its last unfinished suburban terrace. About every ten minutes or so, the clouds opened and the sun flicked and vanished. He held the collar of his baggy, tweed overcoat humped about his neck. His tongue was trying to double back acrobatically to his uvula. Feeling as lost and forlorn as the grey heron he saw across the road standing by the edge of a wrinkled loch, he halted to compose. '*O long-legged bird by your ruffled lake / Alone as I, as bleak of eye, opaque . . .*' As what? He unguardedly rubbed his under-tongue on a sharp tooth, cursed, the sun winked, and he was confronted by one of destiny's infinite options. It was his moment of strength, of romance, of glamour, of youth, of sunshine on a strange shore. A blink of sunlight fell on a brass plate fastened to the red-brick gate pillar beside him, DR FRANCIS BREEN.

The gate was lined with sheet metal. Right and left of it there was a high cutstone wall backing on a coppice of rain-black macrocarpa that extended over the grassgrown border of the road. The house was not visible. He squeaked the gate open, peered timidly up a short curved avenue at it, all in red brick, tall, turreted and baywindowed. An empty-looking conservatory hooped against one side of it (intended, presumably, for the cultivation of rare orchids). Along the other side, a long veranda (intended, doubtless, to shelter Doctor Francis Breen from Ireland's burning tropical sun). He opened his mouth wide as he gazed, probed with his finger for the sore spot, and found it.

It did not look like a house where anybody would start cutting anybody up. It did not look like a doctor's house at all. It looked more like a gentleman's residence. Although he did remember the American visitor to Dublin who said to him that every Irish surgery looked as if it had been furnished by Dr Watson for Sherlock Holmes. As he cautiously entered the avenue he observed that the gate bore a perpendicular column of five warning signs in blue lettering on white enamel. NO DOGS. NO CANVASSERS. NO HAWKERS. NO CIRCULARS. SHUT THE GATE. He advanced on the house, his fists clenched inside his overcoat pockets, his eyebrows lifted to indicate his contempt for all doctors. Twice on the way to the front door he paused, as if to admire the grounds, really to assure himself that no dog had failed to read the NO DOGS sign: a born cityman, he feared all living animals. He was very fond of them in poetry. He took the final step upwards to the stained glass door, stretched out his index finger, to tip, to tempt, to test, to press the brass bell-knob. (An enamel sign beneath it said, TRADESMEN TO THE REAR.) His mother had spoken of a deficiency. She had also mentioned pills. He would ask this sawbones for a pill, or for a soothing bottle. He would not remove his shirt for him. And he would positively refuse to let down his pants. 'Where,' he foresaw himself roaring, 'do you think I have this boil?'

A shadow appeared behind the door. He looked speculatively over his glasses at the servant who partly opened it. She was grey and settled, but not old, dressed in black bombazine, wearing a white starched apron with shoulder frills. When he asked for the doctor she immediately flung the door wide open as if she had been eagerly expecting him for years and years; then, limping eagerly ahead of him, dot and carry one down a softly upholstered corridor, she showed him into what she called 'the dachtar's sargery,' quacking all about 'what an ahful co-eld dayeh it iss Gad bliss itt' in what he had already scornfully come to recognize as the ducks' dialect of this sodden, mist-shotten dung-heap of the Shannon's delta.

Left to himself he had time only to be disturbed by the sight of one, two, three barometers side by side on the wall, and one, two, three, four clocks side by side on the mantelpiece; relieved by an opposite wall lined with books; and enchanted by a dozen daintily tinted lithographs of flying moths and half a dozen hanging glass cases displaying wide-winged butterflies pinned against blue skies, when the door was slammed open by a tall, straight, white-haired, handsome, military-looking man, his temper at boiling point, his voice of the barrack-square, the knuckles of his fist white on the doorknob as if he were as eager to throw out his visitor as his Bombazine had been to welcome him in. Morgan noted that his eyes were quiet as a novice of nuns, and that his words were as polite, and remembered hearing somewhere that when the Duke of Wellington gave his order for the final charge at Waterloo his words to his equerry had been, 'The Duke of Wellington presents his compliments to Field Marshal von Blücher and begs him to be so kind as to charge like blazes.'

'Well, sir?' the doctor was saying. 'Would you be so kind as to tell me what you mean by entering my house in this cavalier fashion? Are you an insurance salesman? Are you distributing circulars? Are you promoting the Encyclopaedia Britannica? Are you a hawker? A huckster? A Jehovah's Witness?'

At these words Morgan's eyes spread to the rims of his lake-size glasses. He felt a heavenly sunlight flooding the entire room. He raised two palms of exultant joy. More than any other gift of life, more than drink, food, girls, books, nicotine, coffee, music, more even than poetry and his old mother (whom he thought of, and saw through, as if she were a stained glass image of the Mother of God), he adored all cranks, fanatics, eccentrics and near-lunatics, always provided that they did not impinge on his personal comfort, in which case he would draw a line across them as fast as a butcher cuts off a chicken's head. More than any other human type he despised all men of good character, all solid citizens, all well-behaved social men, all mixers, joiners, hearty fellows and jolly good chaps, always pro-

vided that he did not require their assistance in his profession as
librarian, in which case he would cajole them and lard them and
lick them like a pander, while utterly despising himself, and his
job, for having to tolerate such bores for one moment. But,
here, before his eyes was a figure of purest gold. If there were
any other such splendid crackpots in L— then this was heaven,
nor was he ever to be out of it.

'But,' he protested gaily, 'you are a doctor! I have a gumboil!
We are the perfect match.'

The old man moaned as if he had been shot through by an
arrow of pain.

'It is true that I am, by letters patent, a man licensed to
practise the crude invention called medicine. But I have never
practised, I have never desired to practise and I never do intend
to practise medicine. I know very well, sir, what you want me
to do. You want me to look down your throat with an electric
torch and make some such solemn, stupid and meaningless
remark as "You have a streptococcal infection." Well,' he protested, 'I will do nothing of the kind for you. Why should I? It
might be only a symptom. Next week you might turn up with
rheumatic heart disease, or a latent kidney disease, as people
with strep throats have been known to do. You talk airily of a
gumboil. You may well be living in a fool's paradise, sir. Even
supposing I were to swab strep out of your throat and grow it
on a culture medium, what would that tell me about the terrible, manifold, creeping, subtle, lethal disease-processes that
may be going on at this moment in the recesses of your body as
part of that strep infection, or set off by it? The only thing I, or
any other doctor – bluffers and liars that we all are – could
honestly say to you would be the usual evasion. "Gargle with
this bottle three times a day and come back in a week." By
which time Nature or God would have in any case cured you
without our alleged assistance. I know the whole bag of tricks
from the Hippocratic collection, the treatises of Galen and the
Canon of Avicenna down. I suppose you imagine that I spent
all my years in Dublin and Vienna studying medicine. I spent
them studying medicos. I am a neurologist. Or I was a neurologist until I found that what true medicine means is true magic.

Do you know how to remove a wart? You must wait on the roadway to the cemetery until a funeral passes, and say, "Corpse, corpse, take away my wart." And your wart will go, sir! That is true medicine. I believe in miracles because I have seen them happen. I believe in God, prayer, the imagination, the destiny of the Irish, our bottomless racial memory – and in nothing else.'

Morgan's left hand was circling his belly in search of manifold, creeping, secret diseases.

'But, surely to God, doctor,' he whined, 'medical science can do *something* for a gumboil?'

'Aha! I know what you're up to now. X-rays! That's the mumbo-jumbo every patient wants. And neither will I suggest, as you would probably like me to suggest, that you should go to hospital. All you would do there would be either to pass your infection to some other patient or pick up his infection from him. I will have nothing to do with you, sir. And please keep your distance. I don't want your beastly infection. If you want to mess about with your gumboil you will have to go to a doctor. If you wish me to pray for your gumboil I will pray for it. But I refuse to let you or anybody else turn me into the sort of mountebank who pretends he can cure any tradesman's sore toe or any clerk's carbuncle in one second with a stroke of his pen and a nostrum from the chemist's shop. Good afternoon to you, sir. You are now in the hands of God!'

Morgan, stung by arrogance and enraged by fear, roared back a line fit for his memoirs.

'And good afternoon to you, sir! From one who is neither clerk nor tradesman, higgler nor hawker, huckster nor hound-dog but, by God's grace, a poet whose poems will live long after,' hand waving, 'your butterflies have been devoured by the jaws of your moths.'

The old man's rage vanished like a ghost at cockcrow. He closed the door gently behind him.

'A poet?' he asked quietly. 'Now, this is most interesting.' Courteously he indicated a chair. 'Won't you sit down? Your name is?'

'Morgan Myles,' Morgan Myles boomed as if he were a majordomo announcing Lord Byron.

'Mine is Francis Breen. Yours is more euphonious. I can see it already on your first book of verses. But a poet should have three names. Like American politicians. Percy Bysshe Shelley. George Gordon Byron. Thomas Stearns Eliot. William Butler Yeats. Ella Wheeler Wilcox. Richard Milhous Nixon. You have a second name? Taken at your Confirmation? Arthur? There we have it! *First Poems.* By Morgan Arthur Myles!'

Morgan, like most men who are adept at flattering others, could never resist flattery himself. He waggled his bottom like a dog. His grin was coy but cocksure. Three minutes later the doctor was tenderly parting his lips and illuminating the inside of his mouth. He extinguished the torch. He lifted his eyes and smiled into Morgan's.

'Well, Doc?' Morgan asked fearfully. 'What did you see there?'

'You are not even,' his new-found friend smiled, 'about to give birth to a couplet. Just a blister.' He sat to his desk. 'I will give you a prescription for a gargle. Rinse your mouth with this three times a day. And come back to me in a week. But if you wish to get better sooner come sooner, any evening for a drink and a chat. I have no friends in L—.'

'Nor have I!'

Within a week they were bosom cronies.

From start to finish it was a ridiculous friendship. Indeed, from that day onwards, to the many of us who saw them every day after lunch walking along O'Connell Street arm in arm like father and son, or nose to nose like an ageing ward boss with a young disciple, it seemed an unnatural business. Can the east wind, we asked one another in wonder, lie down with the west wind? A cormorant mate with a herring? A heron with a hare? An end with a beginning? We gave their beautiful friendship three months. As a matter of fact we were only two years and eleven months out.

Even to look at they were a mismatch: the doctor straight and spare as a spear, radiating propriety from every spiky bone of his body, as short of step as a woman, and as carefully dressed from his wide-brimmed bowler hat to the rubber tip of his mottled, gold-headed malacca cane; the poet striding beside

him, halting only to swirl his flabby tweeds; his splendid hydro-
cephalic head stretched behind his neck like a balloon; his
myopic eyes glaring at the clouds over the roofs through the
thick lenses of his glasses; a waterfall of black hair permanently
frozen over his left eye, his big teeth laughing, his big voice
booming, he looked for all the world like a peasant Yeats in a
poor state of health. The only one of us who managed to produce any sort of explanation was our amateur psychiatrist,
Father Tim Buckley, and we never took him seriously anyway.
He said, with an episcopal *sprinkle me O Lord with hyssop*
wave of his hand, 'They have invented one another.'

Now, we knew from experience that there was only one way
to handle Tim Buckley. If he said some fellow was a homosexual because he had fallen in love with his hobbyhorse when
he was five you had to say at once, 'But, Tim, why did he fall in
love with his hobbyhorse when he was five?' If he said that it
was because the poor chap hated his mother and loved his
father you had to say, at once, 'But, Tim, why did he hate his
ma and love his da?' If he then said that it was natural for every
child to prefer one parent to another, you had to say at once,
'But, Tim, why . . .' And so on until he lost his temper and shut
up. This time, however, he was ready for our counterattack.

'They have invented one another,' he said, 'for mutual support because they are both silently screaming for freedom. Now
what is the form of slavery from which all human beings most
want to be free?'

'Sex,' we conceded, to save time, knowing our man.

'Passion!' he amended. 'For this agony there are only three
solutions. The first is sin, which,' he grinned, 'I am informed on
the best authority is highly agreeable but involves an awful
waste of time. I mean if you could hang a girl up in the closet
every time you were finished with her that would be very convenient, but. Then there is marriage, which as Shaw said is the
perfect combination of maximum temptation and maximum
opportunity. And there is celibacy of which, I can say with
authority, as the only member of the present company who
knows anything at all about it, that it bestows on man the
qualified freedom of a besieged city where one sometimes has to

eat rats. Of our two friendly friends the older man needs approval for his lifelong celibacy. The younger man needs encouragement to sustain his own. Or so they have chosen to imagine. In fact neither of them really believes in celibacy at all. Each has not only invented the other. He has invented himself.'

Our silence was prolonged.

'Very well,' he surrendered. 'In that case thicken your own plot!'

Of course, we who had known Frank Breen closely ever since we were kids together in L—, knew that there was nothing mysterious about him: he had simply always been a bit balmy, even as a four-eyed kid. When his parents sent him to school in England we saw much less of him; still less when he went to Dublin for his M.B., and from there on to Austria for his M.D. After he came back to L— to settle down for life in the old Breen house on the Dublin Road on the death of his father, old Doctor Frank, and of his mother, we hardly saw him at all. We knew about him only by hearsay, chiefly through the gossip of his housekeeper, Dolly Lynch, passed on to Claire Coogan, Father Tim Buckley's housekeeper, and gleefully passed on by him to the whole town.

That was how the town first heard that the brass plate on his gate pillar – his father's, well polished by chamois and dulled by weather – would never again mean that there was a doctor behind it; about his four clocks and his three barometers; about his collection of moths and butterflies; about the rope ladder he had coiled in a red metal box under every bedroom window; about his bed always set two feet from the wall lest a bit of cornice should fall on his head during the night; about the way he looked under the stairs for hidden thieves every night before going to bed; that his gold-knobbed malacca cane contained a sword; that he never arrived at the railway station less than half an hour before his train left; that he hung his pyjamas on a clothes hanger; had handmade wooden trees for every pair of his handmade boots; that he liked to have his bootlaces washed and ironed; that his vest-pocket watch told the time, the date, the day, the year, the points of the compass, and contained an

alarm buzzer that he was always setting to remind him of something important he wanted to do later on, but whose nature he
could never remember when the buzzer hummed over his left
gut – very much the way a wife will leave her wedding ring at
night on her dressing-table to remind her in the morning of
something that by then she has incontinently forgotten.

So! A bit odd. Every club in the world must have elderly
members like him – intelligent and successful men of whose
oddities the secretary will know one, the headwaiter another,
the bartender a third, their fellow members smile at a fourth. It
is only their families, or if they live for a long time in a small
town their townsfolk who will, between them, know the lot.
Frank Breen might have gone on in his harmless, bumbling way
to the end of his life if that brass plate of his had not winked at
Morgan Myles, and if Father Tim Buckley – was he jealous? –
had not decided to play God.

Not that we ever called him 'Father Tim Buckley.' He was
too close to us, too like one of ourselves for that. We called him
Tim Buckley, or Tim, or even, if the whiskey was fluming,
Bucky. He was not at all like the usual Irish priest who is as
warm as toast and as friendly and understanding as a brother
until you come to the sixth commandment, and there is an end
to him. Tim was like a man who had dropped off an international plane at Shannon; not a Spencer Tracy priest from
downtown Manhattan, all cigar and white cuffs, parish com-
puter and portable typewriter, fists and feet, and there is the end
to him; perhaps more like an unfrocked priest from Bolivia or
Brazil, so ungentlemanly in his manners as to have given acute
pain to an Evelyn Waugh and so cheerful in spite of his scars as
to have shocked a Graham Greene; or still more like, among all
other alternatives, a French workers' priest from Liège; or in
other words, as far as we were concerned, the right man in the
right place and as far as the bishop was concerned, a total
disaster. He was handsome, ruddy and full-blooded in a sensual
way, already so heavy in his middle thirties that he had the
belly, the chins and (when he lost his temper) something of the
voracity of Rodin's ferocious statue of Balzac in his dressing-

gown; but he was most himself when his leaden-lidded eyes glistened with laughter, and his tiny mouth, crushed between the peonies of his cheeks, reminded you of a small boy whistling after his dog, or of some young fellow saucily making a kiss-mouth across the street to his girl. His hobby was psychoanalysis.

His analysis of the doctor was characteristic. He first pointed out to us, over a glass of malt, the sexual significance of pocket watches, so often fondled and rubbed between the fingers. He merely shrugged at the idea of ladders unfolding from red containers, and said that swords being in sword sticks needed no comment. Clocks and barometers were merely extensions of pocket watches. (The wristwatch, he assured us, was one of the great sexual revolutions of our age – it brought everything out in the open.) But, above all, he begged us to give due attention to Frank Breen's mother complex – evident in his love of seclusion behind womblike walls, dark trees, a masked gate; and any man must have a terrible hate for his father who mockingly leaves his father's brass plate on a pillar outside his home while publicly refusing to follow his father's profession inside it. ('By the way, can we ignore that NO DOGS sign?') The looking for thieves under the stairs at night, he confessed, puzzled him for the moment. Early arrival for trains was an obvious sign of mental insecurity. 'Though, God knows,' laughing in his fat, 'any man who doesn't feel mentally insecure in the modern world must be out of his mind.' As for this beautiful friendship, that was a classical case of Narcissism: the older man in love with an image of his own lost and lonely youth.

'Any questions?'

No wonder he was the favourite confessor of all the nubile girls in town, not (or not only) because they thought him handsome but because he was always happy to give them the most disturbing explanations for their simplest misdemeanours. 'I kissed a boy at a dance, Father,' they would say to some other priest and, as he boredly bade them say three Hail Marys for their penance, they would hear the dark slide of the confessional move dismissively across their faces. Not so with Father Tim! He would lean his cheek against the grille and whisper, 'Now, my dear child, in itself a kiss is an innocent and beautiful act. Therefore the only reason prompting you to confess it as a sin must refer to the manner in which the kiss was given and the spirit in which it was received, and in this you may be very wise. Because, of course, when we say *kiss*, or *lips*, we may – one never knows for certain – be thinking of something quite different . . .' His penitents would leave his box with their faces glowing, and their eyes dazed. One said that he made her feel like a Magdalen with long floating hair. Another said he made her want to go round L— wearing a dark veil. A third (who was certain to come to a bad end) said he had revealed to her the *splendeurs et misères de l'amour.* And a fourth, clasping her palms with delight, giggled that he was her Saint Rasputin.

We who met him in our homes, with a glass in his fist and his Roman collar thrown aside, did not worry about what he told our daughters. We had long since accepted him as an honest, innocent, unworldly man who seemed to know a lot about sex-in-the-head – and was always very entertaining about it – but who knew sweet damn all about love-in-the-bed, not to mention love at about eleven o'clock at night when your five kids are asleep and the two of you are so edgy from adding up the household accounts that by the time you have decided once again that the case is hopeless all 'to go to bed' means is to go sound asleep. But we did worry about him. He was so outspoken, so trustful of every stranger, had as little guard over his tongue as a sailor ashore, that we could foresee the day when his bishop would become so sick of getting anonymous letters about him that he would shanghai him to some remote punishment-curacy on the backside of Slievenamuck.

We would try to frighten him into caution by telling him that he would end up there, exiled to some spot so insignificant that it would not be marked even on one of those nostalgic one-inch-to-the-mile British Ordnance maps of 1899 that still – indifferent to the effects of time and history, of gunshot and revolution – record every burned out constabulary barracks, destroyed mansion, abandoned branch-railway, eighteenth century 'inn,' disused blacksmith's hovel, silenced windmill, rook-echoing granary or 'R. C. Chapel,' where, we would tell him, is where our brave Bucky would then be, in a baldface presbytery, altitude 1,750 feet, serving a cement-faced chapel, beside an anonymous crossroads, without a tree in sight for ten miles, stuck for life as curator, nurse and slave of some senile parish priest. He would just raise his voice to spit scorn at us; like the night he gobbled us up in a rage:

'And,' he roared, 'if I can't say what I think how the hell am I going to live? Am I free or am I not free? Am I to lie down in the dust and be gagged and handcuffed like a slave? Do ye want me to spend my whole life watching out for traffic signs? Falling rocks! Narrowing Road! Cul-de-sac! Stop! My God, are ye men or are ye mice?'

'Mice!' we roared back with one jovial voice and dispelled the tension in laughter so loud that my wife looked up in fright at the ceiling and said, 'Sssh! Ye bastards! If ye wake the kids I'll make every one of ye walk the floor with them in yeer arms till three in the morning. Or do ye think ye're starting another revolution in yeer old age?'

'We could do worse,' Tim smiled into his double chin.

Whenever he smiled like that you could see the traffic signs lying right and left of him like idols overthrown.

It was a Sunday afternoon in May. The little island was deserted. He was lying on the sunwarmed grass between the other two, all three on their backs, in a row, their hats on their faces. They were neither asleep nor awake. They were breathing as softly as the lake at their feet. They had driven at their ease that morning to the east side of the lake past the small village of Mountshannon, now looking even smaller across the level water, rowed to the island (Tim Buckley at the oars), delighted to find every hillocky green horizon slowly bubbling with cumulus clouds. They had inspected the island's three ruined churches, knee-deep in nettles and fern, and its tenth-century Round Tower that had stood against the morning sun as dark as a factory chimney. They had photographed the ruins, and one another, and then sat near the lake and the boat to discuss the excellent lunch that Dolly Lynch always prepared for 'the young maaaster' on these Sunday outings: her cold chicken and salad, her handmade mayonnaise, her own brown bread and butter, the bottle of Liebfraumilch that Frank had hung by a string in the lake to cool while they explored the island, her double roasted French coffee, flavoured, the way the maaaster always liked it, with chicory and a suspicion of cognac. It was half an hour since they had lain back to sleep. So far everything about the outing had been perfect. No wonder Morgan had jackknifed out of bed that morning at eight o'clock, and Frank Breen wakened with a smile of special satisfaction.

Before Morgan came, exactly two years and eleven months ago, it had been the doctor's custom, at the first call of the cuckoo, to take off now and again (though never too often to establish a precedent), on especially fine Sundays like this, with Father Timothy Buckley in Father Timothy's roomy second-hand Peugeot – Frank did not drive – in search of moths and butterflies, or to inspect the last four walls, perhaps the last three walls, of some eighth-century Hiberno-Romanesque churchlet, or the rotting molar of some Norman castle smelling of cow dung, purple mallow, meadowsweet and the woodsmoke of the last tinkers who had camped there. After Morgan came he had begun to drive off every fine Sunday with Morgan in Morgan's little Ford Prefect. Still, *noblesse oblige*, and also if the journey promised to be a rather long one, he had about twice a year suggested to Morgan that they might invite Father Timothy to join them; and Tim had always come, observing with amusement that they indulgently allowed him to bring his own car, and that they would, after loud protestations, allow him to do all the driving, and that he also had to persuade them forcibly to allow him to pack the luggage on the seat beside him, so as to leave plenty of room – at this point they would all three laugh with the frankest irony – for their lordships' bottoms in the soft and roomy rear of the Peugeot. This luggage consisted of Frank's two butterfly nets, in case one broke, three binoculars and three cameras, one for each, two umbrellas for himself and Morgan, the bulging lunch basket for them all, two foam-rubber cushions, one for his poor old back, one for Morgan's poor young back, and a leather-backed carriage rug so that the dear boy should not feel the cold of the grass going up through him while he was eating his lunch and enjoying – as he was now enjoying – his afternoon siesta.

Retired, each one, into his own secret shell of sleep, they all three looked as dead as they would look in fifteen years' time in one of the photographs they had just taken of themselves. The day had stopped. The film of the climbing towers of clouds had stopped. The lake was silent. The few birds and the three cows they had seen on the island were dozing. Thinking had stopped. Their three egos had stopped. Folk tales say that when a man is asleep on the grass like that, a tiny lizard may creep into his mouth, devour his tongue and usurp its power. After about an hour of silence and dozing some such lizard spoke from the priest's mouth. Afterwards he said that he had been dreaming of the island's hermits, and of what he called the shortitude and latitude of life, and of how soon it stops, and that those two selfish bastards beside him were egotistical sinners, too concerned with their comfort as adolescents to assert their dignity as men. 'And I?' he thought with a start, and woke.

'In Dublin last month,' his lizard said hollowly into his hat, 'I saw a girl on a horse on a concrete street.'

'What?' Morgan asked drowsily, without stirring.

'A girl on a horse,' Tim said, removing his hat, and beholding the glorious blue sky. 'It was the most pathetic sight I ever saw.'

'Why pathetic?' Morgan asked, removing his hat and seeing the blue Pacific sweep into his ken.

'She was riding on a concrete street, dressed as if she was riding to hounds. The fantasy of it was pathetic. Miles away from green fields. But all the girls are gone mad on horses nowadays. I wish somebody would tell them that all they're doing is giving the world a beautiful example of sexual transference. They have simply transferred their natural desire for a man to a four-legged brute.'

'Balderdash,' said Morgan, and put back his hat as Frank patiently lifted his to ask the blueness what all the poor girls who haven't got horses do to inform the public of their adolescent desires.

'They have cars,' Tim said, and sat up slowly, the better to do battle. Morgan sat up abruptly.

'So,' he demanded, 'every time I drive a car I become a homosexual?'

Tim considered the matter judicially.

'Possibly,' he agreed. 'But not necessarily. There are male cars for women, and female cars for men. For women? Club-man, Escort, Rover, Consort, Jaguar, Triumph. Fill 'em up and drive them at seventy miles an hour! What fun! For men? Giulietta. Whose Romeo? Morris Minor. The word means moor – symbolical desire for a small negress. Mercedes? Actually that is Mrs Benz's name. Also means Our Lady of Mercy. Symbolical desire for a large virgin. Ford Consul? Consuela, Our Lady of Consolations. Volvo? Vulva. Volkswagen. Double V. Symbolical . . .'

'Well of all the filthy minds!' Morgan roared.

The doctor sat up with a sigh. His siesta was ruined. His anger was hot upon his humour and his honour.

'I do think, Father Timothy, that you, as a priest of God . . .'

Tim scrambled to his feet, high above him, black as a wine-tun against the pale sheen of the lake.

'A priest, a presbyter, an elder, a sheikh, an old man, a minister, a pastor of sheep? What does that mean? Something superior, elegant, stainless and remote from life like yourself and Master Poet here? An angel, a seraph, a saint, a mystic, a eunuch, a cherubim, a morning star? Do I look like it? Or like a man fat from eating too much, wheezy from smoking too much, sick and tired from trying to do the job he was called on to do? A priest of God is a man with a bum and a belly, and everything that hangs out of a belly or cleaves it, with the same appetites and desires, thirsts and hungers as the men and women, the boys and the girls he lives and works with. It may be very nice for you to look at us before the altar in Saint Jude's all dressed up in our golden robes, swinging a censer, and to think, "There is heavenly power, there is magic." But I have no power. I'm nothing alone. I merely pretend to a power that is an eternity beyond me. When I was in Rome, as a student, a priest in Southern Italy went mad, ran down to the bakery to turn the whole night's baking into the body of God, and from there to the wine factory to turn every flask and vat of flowing wine into the blood of the Lord. But did he? Of course not. Alone he hadn't the power to make a leaf of basil grow. But I will pretend to any boy or girl who is troubled or in misery that

143

I have all the power in heaven to cure them, do mumbo-jumbo, wave hands, say hocus pocus, anything if it will only give them peace. And if that doesn't work I tell them the truth.'

'You are shouting, Father,' Doctor Frank said coldly.

Tim controlled himself. He sat down again. He laughed.

'Ye don't want to hear the truth. Too busy romanticizing, repressing, rationalizing, running away, when everybody knows the pair of ye think of nothing but women from morning to night! Your moths, Frank, that come out in the twilight, your easy girls, your lights o' love, fluttering against your window-panes? Do you want me to believe that you never wish you could open the window to let one in? I saw you, Morgan, the other day in the library fawning over that unfortunate virgin Simcox, and a child could see what was in the minds of the pair of ye. And what do you think she thinks she's doing every time she goes out to the yard to wash the backside of your car with suds and water? Why don't you be a man, Morgan, and face up to it – one day you'll have to be spliced. It's the common fate of all mankind.'

'It hasn't been yours, Father,' Frank snapped.

'Because I took a vow and kept to it, logically.'

'Pfoo!' Morgan snarled at him. 'You know damned well that logic has as much to do with marriage as it has with music.'

Tim looked at him with the air of a small boy who is thinking what fun it would be to shove his Auntie Kitty down the farm-yard well.

'You know,' he said slyly, 'you should ask Fräulein Keel about that the next time she is playing the Appassionata for you,' and was delighted to observe the slow blush that climbed up Morgan's face and the black frown that drew down the doctor's eyebrows. The silence of his companions hummed. He leaned back.

It was about two months ago since Frau Keel had come to L— with her daughter Imogen and her husband Georg, an electrical engineer in charge of a new German factory at the Shannon Free Airport complex. He was about fifty and a Roman Catholic, which was presumably why he had been chosen for this Irish job. His wife was much younger; blonde, handsome, curlyheaded, well-corseted, with long-lashed eyes like a cow. Hera-eyed, Morgan said; dopey, Frank said; false lashes, Tim Buckley said. She was broad of bosom and bottom, strong-legged as a peasant and as heavy-shouldered, one of those abundant, self-indulgent, flesh-folding bodies that Rubens so loved to paint in their pink skin. Imogen was quite different; small, black-avised, black-haired, her skin like a bit of burned cork. She was a *belle laide* of such intensity, so packed and powerful with femininity that you felt that if you were to touch her with one finger she would hoop her back and spring her arms around you like a trap. Morgan had met her in the library, let her talk about music, found himself invited by her mother to hear her play, and unwisely boasted about it to Tim Buckley.

In the sullen silence he heard the lake sucking the stones of the beach. The clouds were less bright. The doctor said primly that he wanted to try his hand with his butterfly net. Morgan said gruffly that he wanted to take some more pictures before the sun went down. Together they walked away across the island. Tim reached for his breviary and began to read the office of the day. 'Let us then be like newborn children hungry for the fresh milk . . .'

The delicate India paper of his breviary whispered each time he turned a page. Presently a drop of rain splashed on his knuckles. He looked about him. The sun still touched the island but nowhere else. The lake hissed at the shore. He stood on a rock but could see no sign of his companions. Were they colloguing with the seventh century? He packed the lunch basket, rolled up the rugs, loaded the cargo, sat in the stern of the boat, opened an umbrella, lit his pipe and waited. He was sick of them. No doubt when slaves fall in love they feel more free . . .

They returned slowly and silently. Little was said as he rowed them to the mainland, and less on the way back to L— because the rain became a cloudburst, and he was alone peering into it. On previous excursions he had always been invited to dine with them. He knew he would not be this evening: a snub that Morgan aggravated by assuring him that they must all meet soon again 'on a more propitious occasion.' He gave them a cheerful goodbye and drove off along the rain-dancing asphalt.

To the devil with their four-course dinner. His freedom was
more important to him. Anyway there were a dozen houses in
town where the wife would be delighted to give him a plate of
bacon and eggs.

Frank said nothing until he had poured their usual aperitif –
a stout dollop of malt.

'That,' he said as he handed the glass of whiskey to Morgan
deep in the best armchair on the side of the turf fire, 'is probably the last time we shall meet his reverence socially.'

Morgan looked portentously over his glasses at the fire.

'A terrible feeling sometimes assails me,' he said, smacking each
sibilant, 'that Timothy John Buckley has a coarse streak in him.'

Frank took the opposite armchair.

'I would call it a grave lack of tact. Even presuming that La
Keel has not already told him that she is a patient of mine.'

'Imogen?' said Morgan, sitting straight up. 'Good God! Is
there something wrong with her?'

'Imogen? Oh, you mean the child? I was referring to the
mother.'

Morgan sat back.

'Oh, and what's wrong with that old battle-axe? Are you
beginning to take patients?'

Frank frowned.

'I have done my best to avoid it. The lady, and her husband,
ever since they heard that I studied neurology in Vienna, have
been very persistent. As for what is wrong, I should not, ethi-
cally speaking as a doctor, discuss the affairs of any patient but,
in this case, I think I may safely speak to you about the matter.
Aye. Because I can trust you. And Bee. Because there is nothing
whatsoever wrong with the lady.'

'Then why did she come to consult you?'

Frank answered this one even more stiffly.

'She speaks of her cycles.'

Morgan, like an old lady crossing a muddy road, ventured
between the pools of his inborn prudishness, his poetic fastidi-
ousness and his natural curiosity:

'Do you by any chance mean she has some sort of what they
call woman trouble?'

'If you mean the menopause, Madame Keel is much too young for that. She means emotional cycles. Elation-depression. Vitality-debility. Exultation-despair. The usual manic-depressive syndrome. She says that ever since she came to Ireland she has been melancholy.'

'Jaysus! Sure, aren't we all melancholy in Ireland? What I'd say that one needs is a few good balls of malt every day or a dose or two of cod liver oil. If I were you, Frank, I'd pack her off about her business.'

The doctor's body stirred restively.

'I have made several efforts to detach myself. She insists that I give her comfort.'

Morgan looked over his glasses at his friend.

'And what kind of comfort would that be?' he asked cautiously.

'That,' his friend said, a trifle smugly, 'is scarcely for me to say.'

Morgan glared into his glass. For a moment he wished Bucky was there to crash through the ROAD NARROWS sign, the CUL-DE-SAC, the FALLING ROCKS.   -

'It is a compliment to you,' he said soapily.

'I take small pride in it, Morgan. Especially since she tells me that she also gets great comfort from her pastor.'

Morgan rose to his feet, dark as a thundercloud, or as a Jove who had not shaved for a week.

'What pastor?' he demanded in his deepest basso.

'You have guessed it. Our companion of today. The Reverend Timothy Buckley. He also gives great comfort to Herr Keel. And to the girl. He holds sessions.'

Jehovah's thunder-rumble rolled.

'Sessions?'

'It is apparently the latest American-Dutch ecumenical idea. Group confessions.'

'The man,' Morgan boomed, 'must be mad! He is worse than mad. Who was it called him Rasputin? He was born to be hanged! Or shot! Or poisoned! That man is e-e-e-evil. Frank! You must stop this monstrous folly at once. Think of the effect on that innocent poor child.'

'I have no intention whatsoever of interfering,' Frank fluttered. 'It's a family affair. I have no least right to interfere. And I suspect she is not in the least innocent. And she is not a child. She is eighteen.'

'Frank!' Morgan roared. 'Have you NO principles?'

A mistake. It is not a nice question to be asked by anybody. Suppose Morgan had been asked by somebody if he had any principles himself! How does any of us know what his principles are? Nobody wants to have to start outlining his principles at a word of command.

'I begin to fear,' Frank said huffily, 'that in all this you are not thinking of me, nor of Frau Keel, nor of Herr Keel, nor of my principles, nor of any principles whatever but solely of the sexual attractions of Fräulein Keel. She has hairy legs. A well-known sign of potency.'

At which moment of dead silence Dolly Lynch opened the door, put in her flushed face and in her slow, flat, obsequious Shannon voice, said, 'Dinner is i-now-eh sarvedeh, Dachtar.' Her employer glared at her. Why was she looking so flushed? The foul creature had probably been outside the door for the last three minutes listening to the rising voices. By tomorrow the thing would be all over the town.

They entered the dining-room in silence. She served them in silence. When she went out they maintained silence, or said small polite things like, 'This spring lamb is very tender,' or 'Forced rhubarb?' The silences were so heavy that Morgan felt obliged to retail the entire life of Monteverdi. Immediately after the coffee, in the drawing-room, he said he had better go home to his mother, and, with fulsome thanks for a splendid lunch and a marvellous dinner, he left his friend to his pipe and, if he had any, his principles.

Morgan did not drive directly to his cottage on the Ennis Road. He drove to the library, extracted from the music section a biography of Monteverdi and drove to the Keels' flat in O'Connell Square. It was Frau Keel, majestic as Brünhilde, who opened the door, received the book as if it were a ticket of admission and invited him to come in. To his annoyance he found Buckley half-filling a settee, winking cheerfully at him, smoking a cigar, a coffee in his paw, a large brandy on a small table beside him. Herr Keel sat beside him, enjoying the same pleasures. Through the dining-room door he caught a glimpse of Imogen with her back to him, clearing the dinner table, her oily black hair coiled as usual on either side of her cheeks. As she leaned over the table he saw the dimpled backs of her knees. She was not wearing stockings. The dark down on her legs suggested the untamed forests of the north.

'Aha!' Herr Keel cried, in (for so ponderous a man) his always surprising countertenor. 'It is Mister Myles. You are most welcome. May I offer you a coffee and a good German cigar? We had just begun a most interesting session.'

Morgan beamed and bowed ingratiatingly. He almost clicked his heels in his desire to show his pleasure and to conceal the frightening thought: 'Is this one of Bucky's sessions?' He beamed as he received the cigar and a brandy from Herr Keel, who bowed in return. He bowed as he accepted a coffee from Frau Keel who beamed in return before she went back to her own place on a small sofa of the sort that the French – so he found out next day from a History of Furniture – call a *canapé*, where she was presently joined by Imogen. Thereafter he found that whenever he glanced (shyly) at Frau Keel she was staring anxiously and intently at Buckley, and whenever he glanced (shyly) at Imogen she was looking at himself with a tiny smile of what, crestfallen, he took to be amusement until she raised her hairy eyebrows and slowly shook her midnight head, and he heard a beautiful noise like a bomb exploding inside his chest at the thought that this black sprite was either giving him sympathy or asking sympathy from him. Either would be delightful. But, then, her eyebrows suddenly plunged, she shook her head threateningly, her smile curled, anger and disapproval sullied her already dark eyes.

'As I was saying,' Father Tim was saying, magisterially waving his cigar, 'if adultery is both a positive fact and a relative term, so is marriage. After all, marriage is much more than what The Master of the Sentences called a *conjunctio viri et mulieris*. It is also a union of sympathy and interest, heart and soul. Without these marriage becomes licensed adultery.'

149

'I agree,' Frau Keel sighed. 'But no woman ever got a divorce for that reason.'

Buckley pursed his little mouth into a provocative smile. 'In fact people do divorce for that very reason. Only they call it mental cruelty.'

'Alas,' said Brünhilde, 'according to our church, there is no such sin as mental cruelty and therefore there is no divorce.'

'There are papal annulments,' Herr Keel said to her coldly, 'if you are interested in such things.'

'I am very interested,' she said to him as frigidly, which was not the kind of warm domestic conversation that Morgan had read about in books.

'You were about to tell us, Father Tim,' Imogen said, 'what you consider unarguable grounds for the annulment of a marriage.'

Sickeningly Buckley beamed at the girl; fawningly she beamed back. *She!* The Hyrcanian tigress! Had this obese sensualist mesmerized the whole lot of them? But he could not, as Buckley calmly began to enumerate the impediments to true wedlock, centre his mind on what was being said, so dumbfounded was he to find that nobody but himself seemed to be forming images of the hideous realities of what he now heard. All he could do was to gulp his brandy, as any man of the world might in such circumstances, and struggle to keep his eyes from Imogen's hirsute legs. (Where had he read that Charles XII had a woman in his army whose beard was two feet long?)

'It is not,' Buckley said, 'a true marriage if it has been preceded by rape. It is not a true marriage if either or both parties are certifiable lunatics. It is not,' here he glanced at Keel, 'a genuine marriage if the father marries the daughter,' smiling at Imogen, 'or if the sister marries the brother. It is not marriage if by error either party marries the wrong person, which can happen when a number of people are being married simultaneously. If either party has previously murdered the wife or husband of the other party it is not really a very good marriage. Nor if either party persuades the other party into adultery beforehand by a promise of marriage afterwards. It is not marriage if the male party is impotent both antecedently and

150

perpetually. Nor if a Christian marries a Jew or other heathen . . .'

At which point they all started talking together, Imogen declaring passionately, 'I would marry a Jew if I damn well wanted to,' and Georg Keel demanding, 'How can you prove impotency?', and Frau Keel protesting with ringed fingers, 'Kein Juden! Kein Juden!', Buckley laughingly crying out, 'I agree, I agree,' and Morgan wailing that it was all bureaucratic balderdash, all quashed suddenly into silence by the prolonged ringing of the doorbell. Keel glanced at his watch and said testily, 'Who on earth . . .?' Imogen, unwilling to lose a fraction of the fight, rushed to the door and led in the late-comer. It was the doctor.

Morgan had to admire his comportment. Though he must have been much taken aback to see all his problems personified before him, the old boy did not falter for a moment in his poise and manners. He formally apologized for his late call to Frau Keel, who revealed her delight in his visit by swiftly patting her hair as she passed a mirror, making him sit beside her, fluttering to Imogen to sit beside Morgan, and yielding him a brandy glass between her palms as if it were a chalice. He accepted it graciously, he did not allow it to pass over him, he bowed like a cardinal, he relaxed into the company, legs crossed, as easily as if he were the host and they his guests. Morgan observed that the cuffs of his trousers were wet. He had walked here in the rain. He must be feeling greatly upset.

'Are you a friend of this dirty old doctor?' Imogen whispered rapidly to Morgan.

'I know him slightly. I like you very much, Imogen.'

'He is a vurm!' she whispered balefully. 'You are another vurm. You both turned Father Tim from the door without a meal.'

'Neither,' said Tim, resuming control, 'is it a marriage if it is clandestine, that is, performed secretly.'

'I would marry in secret if I wanted to,' like a shot from Imogen.

'It wasn't my house,' Morgan whispered. 'I wanted him to stay.'

'What does "secret" mean?' Keel asked petulantly.

'I know you lie,' she whispered.

'It means failing to inform your parish priest.'

'That's more bureaucratic fiddlesticks!' Morgan said, and an electric shock ran up his thigh when Imogen patted it approvingly.

'So,' Tim said dryly to him, 'the Empress Josephine thought, but her failure to obey the regulation meant that the Pope was able to allow the Emperor to eject her from his bed and marry again.'

'Then,' Keel agreed, 'it is a wise precaution.'

'It's bosh!' Morgan declared. 'And cruel bosh.'

'Good man!' said Imogen, and gave him another shock, while Frau Keel turned inquiringly to her pastor who said that the rule might be useful to prevent bigamy but was really no reason for dissolving a marriage, whereat she said, 'Then it is bosh!' and her husband, outraged, proclaimed, 'In my house I will allow nobody to say I am defending bosh!'

She waved him aside, clasped her paws, beamed at Father Timothy and cried, 'And now, for adultery!'

'Alas, Madame, adultery by either party is not sufficient cause to annul a marriage.'

'So we women are trapped!'

'While you men,' charged Imogen, glaring around her, 'can freely go your adulterous ways.'

The doctor intervened mildly.

'Happily none of this concerns anybody in this room.'

'How do you know what concerns me?' she challenged, jumping to her feet, her gripped fists by her lean flanks, her prowlike nose pointing about her like a setter. 'I, Imogen Keel, now, at this moment, vant to commit adultery with somebody in this room.'

Morgan covered his face in his hands. O God! The confessions! She means me. What shall I say? That I want to kiss her knees?

'Imogen!' Keel blazed at her. 'I will not permit this. In delicacy! Not to say, in politeness!'

'Please, Georg!' his wife screamed. 'Not again!' She turned to

the company. 'Always I hear this appeal to politeness and delicacy. It is an excuse. It is an evasion. It is an alibi.'

'Aha!' Imogen proclaimed, one hand throwing towards her
father's throat an imaginary flag or dagger. 'But he has always
been excellent at alibis.'

Keel slammed his empty brandy glass on the coffee table so
hard that its stem snapped. 'How fiery she is!' Morgan thought.
What a heroic way she has of rearing her head back to the left
and lifting her opposite eyebrow to the right. A girl like that
would fight for her man to her death – or, if he betrayed her, to
his. Has she, he wondered, hair on her back. Father Tim, amused
by the whole scene, was saying tactfully but teasingly, 'Imogen
there is one other injustice to women that you must hear about.
It is that you will in most countries not be permitted to marry,
no matter how much you protest, until you have arrived at
the age of twelve and your beloved at the age of fourteen.'

She burst into laughter. They all laughed with relief.

'Finally,' he said tristfully, 'priests may not marry at all.'

'They are nevertheless doing so,' the girl commented pertly.

He looked at her, seemed to consider saying something,
drank the last drop of his coffee, and did not say it. Frau Keel
said it for him, compassionately.

'Only by giving up their priesthood.'

'Or more,' he agreed in a subdued voice.

'The whole caboodle,' Imogen mocked.

They talked a little about current examples of priests who
had given up everything. The subject trailed away. Keel looked
at the window. 'Rain,' he sighed, in so weary a voice that the
doctor at once rose, and all the others with him. As the group
dissolved towards the entrance hall of the apartment Morgan
found himself trailing behind with Imogen.

'What have you against the doctor?' he asked her.

'He is just like my father. And I hate my father. The only
good thing I say about your doctor is that he helps my mother
to put up with my father.'

He must drive old Frank home – he must go on helping Frau
Keel; they must talk about the best way to handle Buckley in
future; they must have Georg Keel on one of their excursions; if

the girl was lonely perhaps Keel would like to bring her with them. She was a superb, a wonderful, a marvellous girl, so heroic, so wild, so passionate. The very first thing they must do was to have Buckley to dinner, and maybe Buckley would bring the girl with him . . . Just then he heard Frank ask Keel if it was too late for them to have a brief word together before he left. If this meant the old fool was falling back on some ridiculous, bloody point of principle about treating Frau Keel . . . As he was making his way towards his friend to offer him a lift home Frau Keel absently shook his hand, handed him his hat, opened the door, bade him good night and the door closed on her voice suggesting to Imogen to drive the good Father to his presbytery in her little car. A minute later he was in the street cursing.

There was not a soul in sight. The rain hung like vests around the lamplights of O'Connell Street. When his car refused to start his rage boiled against that stupid cow Marianne Simcox who must have let water (or something) get into the petrol. After many fruitless zizzings from the starter he saw Imogen's little blue car with the priest aboard shoot past in a wake of spray. More zizzings, more pulling at the choke, a long rest to deflood the carburettor and the engine roared into life, just as Keel's Mercedes, with the doc aboard, vanished through the rain towards the bridge and the Dublin road. He circled wildly, followed their taillights, halted twenty yards behind them outside Frank's house, dowsed his lights, saw him get out and Keel drive away. He ran forward to where Frank was unlocking his iron gate, and clutched his arm beseechingly.

'Frank! I simply must talk to you about Buckley. What is he doing to all those people? What is he doing to that Imogen girl? For God's sake what's going on in that Keel family? I won't sleep a wink unless you tell me all you know about them.'

The doctor marvelled at him for a moment and then returned to his unlocking.

'I do not feel disposed,' he said in his haughtiest voice, holding the gate six inches ajar for the length of his reply, 'to discuss such matters at twelve o'clock at night, on an open road, under a downpour of rain, and all the less so since, so far as I can see, nothing is, as you so peculiarly put it, "going on" that is of any interest to me. Everything seems perfectly normal and in order in the Keel family, except that Herr Keel is a total idiot who seems unable to control his wife, that she seems to me to have developed a most unseemly sexual interest in Father Timothy Buckley, that she is intent on divorcing her husband, that their daughter, who is both impertinent and feckless, is a nymphomaniac, who has quite obviously decided to seduce you, and that I am very glad to say that I need never again lay eyes on them for the rest of my natural life. And, now, sir, good night to you.'

With which he entered his drive, banged the metalled gate behind him, and his wet footsteps died into a voice from his front door wailing, 'Oh, dachtar, dachtar! Wait for me! I have the umbrella here for you. You'll be dhrowneded all together with that aaahful rain . . .'

Morgan spat on the gate, turned and raced for his car, which resolutely refused to start. He implored it until its exhausted starter died into the silence of a final click. He got out, kicked its door soundly, and then overwhelmed by all the revelations he had just heard, especially the one about Imogen and himself, he walked home through the empty streets of L—, singing love songs from the *Barber* and *Don Giovanni* at the top of his voice to the summer rain.

One of the more pleasantly disconcerting things about wilful man is that his most table-thumping decisions rarely conclude the matter in hand. There is always time for a further option. Every score is no better than half-time. *Viz:*

1. That July our poor, dear friend Tim Buckley left us for a chin-pimple of a village called Four Noughts (the vulgarization of a Gaelic word meaning Stark Naked) on the backside of Slievenamuck. We loyally cursed His Lordship the bishop, while feeling that he had had no option. For weeks the dogs in the streets had been barking, 'Im-o-gen Keel.' At the farewell party Tim assured us that the bish had neither hand, act nor part in it. He had himself asked His Lordship for a transfer. He asked us to pray for him. He said sadly that he believed he was gone beyond it. The die was cast, the Rubicon crossed, it was the Ides of March, and so forth and so on.

One effect of this event (Dolly Lynch reporting, after her usual survey of her master's wastepaper basket) was that Mister Myles had been invited to dinner with the dachtar at his earliest convenience.

2. That August we heard that Frau Keel was claiming a separation from her husband *a mensa et a thoro*; that she was also applying for a papal annulment of her marriage on the ground of his impotence, which meant that she was ready to swear that Imogen was not his child. Herr Keel, we gathered, had knocked her down, broken one of her ribs with a kick and left for Stuttgart swearing that he would foil her if it cost him his last deutschmark.

Mister Myles was by now dining every week with the doctor, who was also (Dolly Lynch's knuckle suspended outside the dining-room door) seeing Frau Keel regularly, who (Dolly Lynch's hand on the doorknob) was also in constant consultation, through Imogen, with Father Tim Buckley in his exile on Slievenamuck.

3. That September Tim Buckley disappeared from Four Noughts, Imogen Keel disappeared from the Keel flat, and both were reported to have been seen at Shannon Airport boarding a plane for Stockholm. This blow brought us down. Tim's way of living life had been to tell us how to live it. Now that he was starting to live it himself he was no better than any of us. He was the only one of us who had both faced and been free of the world of men, of women, of children, of the flesh. Now we knew that it cannot be done. You must not put your toe into the sea if you do not want to swim in it.

Myles was by now dining with Frank Breen three times a week, friendship glued by gossip.

4. October. Dreadful news from Stuttgart. Herr Keel had accidentally killed himself while cleaning a shotgun. When the news came Morgan was having tea with Frau Keel. She collapsed, calling for the doctor. Morgan drove at once to Frank's house and brought him back to her. For the rest of that month Myles was dining every night with the doctor.

5. By November Dolly Lynch reported that Mister Myles had stopped dining with the doctor but, Mrs Keel, she spat, was

coming as often as 'tree taimes every bluddy wee-uk.' When we heard this we looked at one another. Our eyes said, 'Could it be possible?' We asked Morgan. He was in no doubt about it.

'Buckley was right!' he stormed. 'The man is a sexual maniac! A libertine! A corrupter of women! A traitor and a liar. As that foolish woman will discover before the year is out.'

It was a spring wedding, and the reception was one of the gayest, most crowded, most lavish the town had ever seen. The metal sheeting was gone from the gate, the cypresses cut down, the warning signs inside the gate removed, the brass plate removed, the conservatory packed with flowers, the only drink served was champagne. The doctor became Frank to every Tom and Harry. For the first time we found out that his wife's name was Victorine. With his hair tinted he looked ten years younger. Long before the reception ended he was going around whispering to everybody, as a dead secret, that Victorine was expecting.

6. Morgan, naturally, did not attend the wedding. He took off for the day with Marianne Simcox, and they have since been taking off every fine Sunday in her red Mustang, together with Morgan's mother, in search of faceless churchlets in fallow fields where the only sound is the munching of cattle. His mother prepares the lunch. Marianne reads out his own poems to him. They both feed him like a child with titbits from their fingers. But who knows the outcome of any mortal thing? Buckley – there is no denying it – had a point when he insisted that man's most ingenious invention is man, that to create others we must first imagine ourselves, and that to keep us from wandering, or wondering, in some other direction where a greater truth may lie, we set up all sorts of roadblocks and traffic signals. Morgan has told his Marianne that he has always admired the virginal type. It is enough to put any girl off her stroke. A wink of a brass plate in a country road set him off on one tack. A wink from her might set him off on another. What should she do? Obey his traffic signs, or acknowledge the truth – that he is a born liar – and start showing him a glimpse of thigh?

Heaven help the women of the world, always wondering what the blazes their men's next graven image will be.

How to Write a Short Story

One wet January night, some six months after they had met, young Morgan Myles, our county librarian, was seated in the doctor's pet armchair, on one side of the doctor's fire, digesting the pleasant memory of a lavish dinner, while leafing the pages of a heavy photographic album and savouring a warm brandy. From across the hearth the doctor was looking admiringly at his long, ballooning Gaelic head when, suddenly, Morgan let out a cry of delight.

'Good Lord, Frank! There's a beautiful boy! One of Raphael's little angels.' He held up the open book for Frank to see. 'Who was he?'

The doctor looked across at it and smiled.

'Me. Aged twelve. At school in Mount Saint Bernard.'

'That's in England. I didn't know you went to school in England'.

'Alas!'

Morgan glanced down at twelve, and up at sixty.

'It's not possible, Frank!'

The doctor raised one palm six inches from the arm of his chair and let it fall again.

'It so happened that I was a ridiculously beautiful child.'

'Your mother must have been gone about you. And,' with a smile, 'the girls too.'

'I had no interest in girls. Nor in boys either, though by your smile you seem to say so. But there was one boy who took a considerable interest in me.'

Morgan at once lifted his nose like a pointer. At this period of his life he had rested from writing poetry and was trying to write short stories. For weeks he had read nothing but Maupassant. He was going to out-Maupassant Maupassant. He was

158

going to write stories that would make poor old Maupassant turn as green as the grass on his grave.

'Tell me about it,' he ordered. 'Tell me every single detail.'

'There is nothing to it. Or at any rate, as I now know, nothing abnormal. But, at that age!' – pointing with his pipestem. 'I was as innocent as . . . Well, as innocent as a child of twelve! Funny that you should say that about Raphael's angels. At my preparatory school here – it was a French order – Sister Angélique used to call me her *petit ange*, because, she said, I had *"une tête d'ange et une voix d'ange."* She used to make me sing solo for them at Benediction, dressed in a red soutane, a white lacy surplice and a purple bow tie.

'After that heavenly place Mount Saint Bernard was ghastly. Mobs of howling boys. Having to play games; rain, hail or snow. I was a funk at games. When I'd see a fellow charging me at rugger I'd at once pass the ball or kick for touch. I remember the coach cursing me. "Breen, you're a bloody little coward, there are boys half your weight on this field who wouldn't do a thing like that." And the constant discipline. The constant priestly distrust. Watching us like jail warders.'

'Can you give me an example of that?' Morgan begged. 'Mind you, you could have had that, too, in Ireland. Think of Clongowes. It turns up in Joyce. And he admired the Jesuits!'

'Yes, I can give you an example. It will show you how innocent I was. A month after I entered Mount Saint Bernard I was so miserable that I decided to write to my mother to take me away. I knew that every letter had to pass under the eyes of the Prefect of Discipline, so I wrote instead to Sister Angélique asking her to pass on the word to my mother. The next day old Father George Lee – he's long since dead – summoned me to his study. "Breen!" he said darkly, holding up my unfortunate letter, "you have tried to do a very underhand thing, something for which I could punish you severely. Why did you write this letter in *French*?" ' The doctor sighed. 'I was a very truthful little boy. My mother had brought me up to be truthful simply by never punishing me for anything I honestly owned up to. I said, "I wrote it in French, sir, because I hoped you wouldn't be able to understand it." He turned his face away from me but I could tell from his shoulders that he was laughing. He did not cane me, he just tore up the letter, told me never to try to deceive him again, and sent me packing with my tail between my legs.'

'The old bastard!' Morgan said sympathetically, thinking of the lonely little boy.

'No, no! He was a nice old man. And a good classical scholar, I later discovered. But that day as I walked down the long corridor, with all its photographs of old boys who had made good, I felt the chill of the prison walls!'

'But this other boy?' Morgan insinuated. 'Didn't his friendship help at all?'

The doctor rose and stood with his back to the fire staring fixedly in front of him.

(He rises, Morgan thought, his noble eyes shadowed. No! God damn it, no! Not noble. Shadowed? Literary word. Pensive? Blast it, that's worse. 'Pensive eve!' Romantic fudge. His eyes are dark as a rabbit's droppings. That's got it! In his soul ... Oh, Jase!)

'Since I was so lonely I suppose he *must* have helped. But he was away beyond me. Miles above me. He was a senior. He was the captain of the school.'

'His name,' Morgan suggested, 'was, perhaps, Cyril?'

'We called him Bruiser. I would rather not tell you his real name.'

'Because he is still alive,' Morgan explained, 'and remembers you vividly to this day.'

'He was killed at the age of twenty.'

'In the war! In the heat of battle.'

'By a truck in Oxford. Two years after he went up there from Mount Saint Bernard. I wish I knew what happened to him in those two years. I can only hope that before he died he found a girl.'

'A girl? I don't follow. Oh yes! Of course, yes, I take your point.'

(He remembers with tenderness? No. With loving kindness! No! With benevolence? Dammit, no! With his wonted chivalry to women? But he remembered irritably that the old man sitting opposite to him was a bachelor. And a virgin?)

'What happened between the pair of ye? "Brothers and companions in tribulation on the isle that is called Patmos"?'

The doctor snorted.

'Brothers? I have told you I was twelve. Bruiser was eighteen. The captain of the school. Captain of the rugby team. Captain of the tennis team. First in every exam. Tops. Almost a man. I looked up to him as a shining hero. I never understood what he saw in me. I have often thought since that he may have been amused by my innocence. Like the day he said to me, "I suppose, Rosy," that was my nickname, I had such rosy cheeks, "suppose you think you are the best-looking fellow in the school?" I said, "No, I don't, Bruiser. I think there's one fellow better-looking than me, Jimmy Simcox." '

'Which he, of course, loyally refused to believe!'

The old doctor laughed heartily.

'He laughed heartily.'

'A queer sense of humour!'

'I must confess I did not at the time see the joke. Another day he said, "Would you like, Rosy, to sleep with me?" '

Morgan's eyes opened wide. Now they were getting down to it.

'I said, "Oh, Bruiser, I don't think you would like that at all. I'm an awful chatterbox in bed. Whenever I sleep with my Uncle Tom he's always saying to me, 'Will you, for God's sake, stop your bloody gabble and let me sleep.' " He laughed for five minutes at that.'

'I don't see much to laugh at. He should have sighed. I will make him sigh. Your way makes him sound a queer hawk. And nothing else happened between ye but this sort of innocent gabble? Or are you keeping something back? Hang it, Frank, there's no story at all in this!'

'Oh, he used sometimes take me on his lap. Stroke my bare knee. Ruffle my hair. Kiss me.'

'How did you like that?'

'I made nothing of it. I was used to being kissed by my elders – my mother, my bachelor uncles, Sister Angélique, heaps of people.' The doctor laughed. 'I laugh at it now. But his first kiss! A few days before, a fellow named Calvert said to me, "Hello, pretty boy, would you give me a smuck?" I didn't know what a

smuck was. I said, "I'm sorry, Calvert, but I haven't got one."
The story must have gone around the whole school. The next
time I was alone with Bruiser he taunted me. I can hear his
angry, toploftical English voice. "You are an innocent mug,
Rosy! A smuck is a kiss. Would you let *me* kiss you?" I said,
"Why not?" He put his arm around my neck in a vice and
squashed his mouth to my mouth, hard, sticky. I thought I'd
choke. "O Lord," I thought, "this is what he gets from playing
rugger. This is a rugger kiss." And, I was thinking, "His poor
mother! Having to put up with this from him every morning
and every night." When he let me go, he said, "Did you like
that?" Not wanting to hurt his feelings I said, imitating his
English voice, "It was all right, Bruiser! A bit like ruggah, isn't
it?" He laughed again and said, "All right? Well, never mind. I
shan't rush you." '

Morgan waved impatiently.

'Look here, Frank! I want to get the background to all this.
The telling detail, you know. "The little actual facts" as Stend-
hal called them. You said the priests watched you all like hawks.
The constant discipline, you said. The constant priestly distrust.
How did ye ever manage to meet alone?'

'It was very simple. He was the captain of the school. The
apple of their eye. He could fool them. He knew the ropes.
After all, he had been there for five years. I remember old
Father Lee saying to me once, "You are a very lucky boy,
Breen, it's not every junior that the captain of the school would
take an interest in. You ought to feel very proud of his friendship." We used to have a secret sign about our meetings. Every
Wednesday morning when he would be walking out of chapel,
leading the procession, if that day was all right for us he used to
put his right hand in his pocket. If for any reason it was not all
right he would put his left hand in his pocket. I was always on
the aisle of the very last row. Less than the dust. Watching for
the sign like a hawk. We had a double check. I'd then find a
note in my overcoat in the cloakroom. All it ever said was, "The
same place." He was very careful. He only took calculated
risks. If he had lived he would have made a marvellous poli-
tician, soldier or diplomat.'

'And where would ye meet? I know! By the river. Or in the woods? "Enter these enchanted woods ye who dare!" '

'No river. No woods. There was a sort of dirty old trunk room upstairs, under the roof, never used. A rather dark place with only one dormer window. It had double doors. He used to lock the outside one. There was a big cupboard there – for cricket bats or something. "If anyone comes," he told me, "you will have time to pop in there." He had it all worked out. Cautious man! I had to be even more cautious, stealing up there alone. One thing that made it easier for us was that I was so much of a junior and he was so very much of a senior, because, you see, those innocent guardians of ours had the idea that the real danger lay between the seniors and the middles, or the middles and the juniors, but never between the seniors and the juniors. They kept the seniors and the middles separated by iron bars and stone walls. Any doctor could have told them that in cold climates like ours the really dangerous years are not from fifteen up but from eighteen to anything, up or down. It simply never occurred to them that any senior could possibly be interested in any way in a junior. I, of course, had no idea of what he was up to. I had not even reached the age of puberty. In fact I honestly don't believe he quite knew himself what he was up to.'

'But, dammit, you must have had some idea! The secrecy, the kissing, alone, up there in that dim, dusty box-room, not a sound but the wind in the slates.'

'Straight from the nuns? *Un petit ange?* I thought it was all just pally fun.'

Morgan clapped his hands.

'I've got it! An idyll! Looking out dreamily over the fields from that dusty dormer window? That's it, that's the ticket. Did you ever read that wonderful story by Maupassant – it's called *An Idyll* – about two young peasants meeting in a train, a poor, hungry young fellow who has just left home, and a girl with her first baby. He looked so famished that she took pity on him like a mother, opened her blouse and gave him her breast. When he finished he said, "That was my first meal in three days." Frank! You are telling me the most beautiful story I ever heard in my whole life.'

'You think so?' the doctor said morosely. 'I think he was going through hell all that year. At eighteen? On the threshold of manhood? In love with a child of twelve? That is, if you will allow that a youth of eighteen may suffer as much from love as a man twenty years older. To me the astonishing thing is that he did so well all that year at his studies and at sports. Killing the pain of it, I suppose? Or trying to? But the in between? What went on in the poor devil in between?'

Morgan sank back dejectedly.

'I'm afraid this view of the course doesn't appeal to me at all. All I can see is the idyll idea. After all, I mean, nothing happened!'

Chafing, he watched his friend return to his armchair, take another pipe from the rack, fill it slowly and ceremoniously from a black tobacco jar and light it with care. Peering through the nascent smoke, Morgan leaned slowly forward.

'Or did something happen?'

'Yes,' the doctor resumed quietly. 'Every year, at the end of the last term, the departing captain was given a farewell dinner. I felt sad that morning because we had not met for a whole week. And now, in a couple of days we would be scattered and I would never see him again.'

'Ha, ha! You see, you too were in love!'

'Of course I was, I was hooked,' the doctor said with more than a flicker of impatience. 'However . . . That Wednesday as he passed me in the chapel aisle he put his right hand in his pocket. I belted off at once to my coat hanging in the cloakroom and found his note. It said, "At five behind the senior tennis court." I used always to chew up his *billet doux* immediately I read it. He had ordered me to. When I read this one my mouth went so dry with fear that I could hardly swallow it. He had put me in an awful fix. To meet alone in the box-room was risky enough, but for anybody to climb over the wall into the seniors' grounds was unheard of. If I was caught I would certainly be flogged. I might very well be expelled. And what would my mother and father think of me then? On top of all I was in duty bound to be with all the other juniors at prep at five o'clock, and to be absent from studies without permission was another crime of the first order. After lunch I went to the Prefect of Studies and asked him to excuse me from prep because I had an awful headache. He wasn't taken in one bit. He just ordered me to be at my place in prep as usual. The law! Orders! Tyranny! There was only one thing for it, to dodge prep, knowing well that whatever else happened later I would pay dearly for it.'

'And what about him? He knew all this. And he knew that if *he* was caught they couldn't do anything to him. The captain of the school? Leaving in a few days? It was very unmanly of him to put you to such a risk. His character begins to emerge, and not very pleasantly. Go on!'

The doctor did not need the encouragement. He looked like a small boy sucking a man's pipe.

'I waited until the whole school was at study and then I crept out into the empty grounds. At that hour the school, the grounds, everywhere, was as silent as the grave. Games over. The priests at their afternoon tea. Their charges safely under control. I don't know how I managed to get over that high wall, but when I fell scrambling down on the other side, there he was. "You're bloody late," he said crossly. "How did you get out of prep? What excuse did you give?" When I told him he flew into a rage. "You little fool!" he growled. "You've balloxed it all up. They'll know you dodged. They'll give you at least ten on the backside for this." He was carrying a cane. Seniors at Saint Bernard's did carry walking-sticks. I'd risked so much for him, and now he was so angry with me that I burst into tears. He put his arms around me – I thought, to comfort me – but after that all I remember from that side of the wall was him pulling down my short pants, holding me tight, I felt something hard, like his cane, and the next thing I knew I was wet. I thought I was bleeding. I thought he was gone mad. When I smelled whiskey I thought, "He is trying to kill me." "Now run," he ordered me, "and get back to prep as fast as you can." '

Morgan covered his eyes with his hand.

'He shoved me up to the top of the wall. As I peered around I heard his footsteps running away. I fell down into the shrubs on the other side and I immediately began to vomit and vomit.

There was a path beside the shrubs. As I lay there puking I saw a black-soutaned priest approaching slowly along the path. He was an old, old priest named Constable. I did not stir. Now, I felt, I'm for it. This is the end. I am certain he saw me but he passed by as if he had not seen me. I got back to the study hall, walked up to the Prefect's desk and told him I was late because I had been sick. I must have looked it because he at once sent me to the matron in the infirmary. She took my temperature and put me to bed. It was summer. I was the only inmate of the ward. One of those evenings of prolonged daylight.'

'You poor little bugger!' Morgan groaned in sympathy.

'A detail comes back to me. It was the privilege of seniors attending the captain's dinner to send down gifts to the juniors' table – sweets, fruit, a cake, for a younger brother or some special protégé. Bruiser ordered a whole white blancmange with a rose cherry on top of it to be sent to me. He did not know I was not in the dining hall so the blancmange was brought up to me in the infirmary. I vomited again when I saw it. The matron, with my more than ready permission, took some of it for herself and sent the rest back to the juniors' table, "with Master Breen's compliments." I am sure it was gobbled greedily. In the morning the doctor saw me and had me sent home to Ireland immediately.'

'Passing the buck,' said Morgan sourly, and they both looked at a coal that tinkled from the fire into the fender.

The doctor peered quizzically at the hissing coal.

'Well?' he slurred around his pipestem. 'There is your lovely idyll.'

Morgan did not lift his eyes from the fire. Under a downdraught from the chimney a few specks of grey ashes moved clockwise on the worn hearth. He heard a car hissing past the house on the wet macadam. His eyebrows had gone up over his spectacles in two Gothic arches.

'I'm afraid,' he said at last, 'it is no go. Not even a Maupassant could have made a story out of it. And Chekhov wouldn't have wanted to try. Unless the two boys lived on, and on, and met years afterwards in Moscow or Yalta or somewhere, each with a wife and a squad of kids, and talked of everything except

166

their schooldays. You are sure you never did hear of him, or from him, again?'

'Never! Apart from the letter he sent with the blancmange and the cherry.'

Morgan at once leaped alive.

'A letter? Now we are on to something! What did he say to you in it? Recite every word of it to me! Every syllable. I'm sure you have not forgotten one word of it. No!' he cried excitedly. 'You have kept it. Hidden away somewhere all these years. Friendship surviving everything. Fond memories of . . .'

The doctor sniffed.

'I tore it into bits unread and flushed it down the W.C.'

'Oh, God blast you, Frank!' Morgan roared. 'That was the climax of the whole thing. The last testament. The final revelation. The summing up. The *document humain*. And you "just tore it up!" Let's reconstruct it. "Dearest Rosy, As long as I live I will never forget your innocence, your sweetness, your . . ."'

'My dear boy!' the doctor protested mildly. 'I am sure he wrote nothing of the sort. He was much too cautious, and even the captain was not immune from censorship. Besides, sitting in public glory at the head of the table? It was probably a place-card with something on the lines of, "All my sympathy, sorry, better luck next term." A few words, discreet, that I could translate any way I liked.'

Morgan raised two despairing arms.

'If that was all the damned fellow could say to you after that appalling experience, he was a character of no human significance whatever, a shallow creature, a mere agent, a catalyst, a cad. The story becomes your story.'

'I must admit I have always looked on it in that way. After all it did happen to me . . . Especially in view of the sequel.'

'Sequel? What sequel? I can't have sequels. In a story you always have to observe unity of time, place and action. Everything happening at the one time, in the same place, between the same people. *The Necklace. Boule de Suif. The Maison Tellier.* The examples are endless. What was this bloody sequel?'

The doctor puffed thoughtfully.

'In fact there were two sequels. Even three sequels. And all of them equally important.'

'In what way were they important?'

'It was rather important to me that after I was sent home I was in the hospital for four months. I could not sleep. I had constant nightmares, always the same one – me running through a wood and him running after me with his cane. I could not keep down my food. Sweating hot. Shivering cold. The vomiting was recurrent. I lost weight. My mother was beside herself with worry. She brought doctor after doctor to me, and only one of them spotted it, an old, blind man from Dublin named Whiteside. He said, "That boy has had some kind of shock," and in private he asked me if some boy, or man, had interfered with me. Of course, I denied it hotly.'

'I wish I was a doctor,' Morgan grumbled. 'So many writers were doctors. Chekhov. William Carlos Williams. Somerset Maugham. A. J. Cronin.'

The doctor ignored the interruption.

'The second sequel was that when I at last went back to Mount Saint Bernard my whole nature changed. Before that I had been dreamy and idle. During my last four years at school I became their top student. I suppose psychologists would say nowadays that I compensated by becoming extroverted. I became a crack cricket player. In my final year I was the college champion at billiards. I never became much good at rugger but I no longer minded playing it and I wasn't all that bad. If I'd been really tops at it, or at boxing, or swimming, I might very well have ended up as captain of the school. Like him.'

He paused for so long that Morgan became alerted again.

'And the third sequel?' he prompted.

'I really don't know why I am telling you all this. I have never told a soul about it before. Even still I find it embarrassing to think about, let alone to talk about. When I left Mount Saint Bernard and had taken my final at the College of Surgeons I went on to Austria to continue my medical studies. In Vienna I fell in with a young woman. The typical blonde fräulein, handsome, full of life, outgoing, wonderful physique, what you might call an outdoor girl, free as the wind, frank as the daylight. She taught me skiing. We used to go mountain climbing together. I don't believe she knew the meaning of the word fear. She was great fun and the best of company. Her name was Brigitte. At twenty-six she was already a woman of the world. I was twenty-four, and as innocent of women as ... as ...'

To put him at his ease Morgan conceded his own embarrassing confession.

'As I am, at twenty-four.'

'You might think that what I am going to mention could not happen to a doctor, however young but, on our first night in bed, immediately she touched my body I vomited. I pretended to her that I had eaten something that upset me. You can imagine how nervous I felt all through the next day wondering what was going to happen that night. Exactly the same thing happened that night. I was left with no option. I told her the whole miserable story of myself and Bruiser twelve years before. As I started to tell her I had no idea how she was going to take it. Would she leave me in disgust? Be coldly sympathetic? Make a mock of me? Instead, she became wild with what I can only call gleeful curiosity. "Tell me more, *mein Schätzerl*," she begged. "Tell me everything! What exactly did he do to you? I want to know it all. This is *wunderbar*. Tell me! Oh do tell me!" I did tell her, and on the spot everything became perfect between us. We made love like Trojans. That girl saved my sanity.'

In a silence Morgan gazed at him. Then coldly:

'Well, of course, this is another story altogether. I mean I don't see how I can possibly blend these two themes together. I mean no writer worth his salt can say things like, "Twelve long years passed over his head. Now read on." I'd have to leave her out of it. She is obviously irrelevant to the main theme. Whatever the hell the main theme is.' Checked by an ironical glance he poured the balm. 'Poor Frank! I foresee it all. You adored her. You wanted madly to marry her. Her parents objected. You were star-crossed lovers. You had to part.'

'I never thought of marrying the bitch. She had the devil's temper. We had terrible rows. Once we threw plates at one another. We would have parted anyway. She was a lovely girl but quite impossible. Anyway, towards the end of that year my father fell seriously ill. Then my mother fell ill. Chamberlain was in Munich that year. Everybody knew the war was coming. I came back to Ireland that autumn. For keeps.'

'But you tried again and again to find out what happened to her. And failed. She was swallowed up in the fire and smoke of war. I don't care what you say, Frank, you *must* have been heartbroken.'

The doctor lifted a disinterested shoulder.

'A student's love affair? Of thirty and more years ago?'

No! He had never inquired. Anyway if she was alive now what would she be but a fat, blowsy old baggage of sixty-three? Morgan, though shocked, guffawed dutifully. There was the real Maupassant touch. In his next story a touch like that! The clock on the mantelpiece whirred and began to tinkle the hour. Morgan opened the album for a last look at the beautiful child. Dejectedly he slammed it shut, and rose.

'There is too much in it,' he declared. 'Too many strands. Your innocence. His ignorance. Her worldliness. Your forgetting her. Remembering him. Confusion and bewilderment. The ache of loss? Loss? *Lost Innocence?* Would that be a theme? But nothing rounds itself off. You are absolutely certain you never heard of him again after that day behind the tennis courts?'

They were both standing now. The rain brightly spotted the midnight window.

'In my first year in Surgeons, about three years after Bruiser was killed, I lunched one day with his mother and my mother at the Shelbourne Hotel in Dublin. By chance they had been educated at the same convent in England. They talked about him. My mother said, "Frank here knew him in Mount Saint Bernard." His mother smiled condescendingly at me. "No, Frank. You were too young to have met him." "Well," I said, "I did actually speak to him a couple of times, and he was always very kind to me." She said sadly, "He was kind to everybody. Even to perfect strangers." '

Morgan thrust out an arm and a wildly wagging finger.

'Now, *there* is a possible shape! Strangers to begin. Strangers to end! What a title! *Perfect Strangers.*' He blew out a long, impatient breath and shook his head. 'But that is a fourth sequel! I'll think about it,' as if he were bestowing a great favour. 'But it isn't a story as it stands. I would have to fake it up a lot. Leave out things. Simplify. Mind you, I could still see it as an idyll. Or I could if only you hadn't torn up his last, farewell letter, which I still don't believe at all said what you said it said. If only we had that letter I bet you any money we could haul in the line and land our fish.'

The doctor knocked out the dottle of his pipe against the fireguard, and throating a yawn looked at the fading fire.

'I am afraid I have been boring you with my reminiscences.'

'Not at all, Frank! By no means! I was most interested in your story. And I do honestly mean what I said. I really will think about it. I promise. Who was it,' he asked in the hall as he shuffled into his overcoat and his muffler and moved out to the wet porch, the tail of his raincoat rattling in the wind, 'said that the two barbs of childhood are its innocence and its ignorance?' He failed to remember. He threw up his hand. 'Ach, to hell with it for a story! It's all too bloody convoluted for me. And to hell with Maupassant, too! That vulgarian over-simplified everything. And he's full of melodrama. A besotted Romantic at heart! Like all the bloody French.'

The doctor peeped out at him through three inches of door. Morgan, standing with his back to the arrowy night, suddenly lit up as if a spotlight had shone on his face.

'I know what I'll do with it!' he cried. 'I'll turn it into a poem about a seashell!'

'About a seashell?'

'Don't you remember?' In his splendid voice Morgan chanted above the rain and wind: – ' *"A curious child holding to his ear | The convolutions of a smoothlipped seashell | To which, in silence hushed ..."* How the hell does it go? *"... his very soul listened to the murmurings of his native sea."* It's as clear as daylight, man! You! Me! Everyone! Always wanting to launch a boat in search of some far-off golden sands. And something or somebody always holding us back. "The Curious Child." *There's* a title!'

'Ah, well!' the doctor said, peering at him blankly. 'There it is! As your friend Maupassant might have said, "*C'est la vie!*" '

'*La vie!*' Morgan roared, now on the gravel beyond the porch, indifferent to the rain pelting on his bare head. 'That trollop? She's the one who always bitches up everything. No, Frank! For me there is only one fountain of truth, one beauty, one perfection. Art, Frank! Art! And bugger *la vie!*'

At the untimely verb the doctor's drooping eyelids shot wide open.

'It is a view,' he said courteously and let his hand be shaken fervently a dozen times.

'I can never repay you, Frank. A splendid dinner. A wonderful story. Marvellous inspiration. I must fly. I'll be writing it all night!' – and vanished head down through the lamplit rain, one arm uplifted triumphantly behind him.

The doctor slowly closed his door, carefully locked it, bolted it, tested it, and prudently put its chain in place. He returned to his sitting-room, picked up the cinder that had fallen into the hearth and tossed it back into the remains of his fire, then stood, hand on mantelpiece, looking down at it. What a marvellous young fellow! He would be tumbling and tossing all night over that story. Then he would be around in the morning apologizing, and sympathizing, saying, 'Of course, Frank, I do realize that it was a terribly sad experience for both of you.'

Gazing at the ashes his whole being filled with memory after memory like that empty vase in his garden being slowly filled by drops of rain.

Liberty

Three men are seated on a low grassy wall opposite the high, white, wide, double, wooden, open gates and porter's lodge of a mental institution a mile from the modest town of B— in the province of D—. Once it was frankly called The Madhouse, later more delicately The Asylum, still later, more accurately, The Mental Hospital, finally, less candidly, Saint Senan's Home. Two of the three men are fat and wear peaked-cap uniforms. The third, thin and tall, wears another kind of uniform, the usual, grey, hirsute, tweed suit, hairy grey cap, woollen shirt and the boots without laces worn by all housebound patients. A few, so-called 'good' patients, who are encouraged to walk freely about the neighbouring town and countryside, dress like you and me. This man is privileged to sit just outside the gates of the Home.

The three men are looking at the ground under their feet, considering whether, without spoiling this favoured spot, it would be feasible to have some gravel spread there as an insurance against the fog, damps and miasmas rising under their boots when the ground tends to become soft and muddy. The patient, answering to the name Mister Cornfield, has just suggested that the low wall would be a more comfortable seat if paved with flagstones. This suggestion meets with a majority disapproval.

'Cold flags,' says the fatter of the attendants, slowly and paternally circling his belly with his open palm, 'could give you piles.'

Mr Cornfield argues quietly that damp grass and damp earth are 'just as conducive to haemorrhoids.'

At this the two attendants begin to discuss the meaning of the words *piles* and *haemorrhoids*. Mr Cornfield, for whose knowl-

173

edgeability and cleverality they entertain a very proper respect
(he was once a journalist) informs them that the word *piles*
comes from Old English and etymologizes from the same
source as the word *pellets*, or as the Spanish form of tennis
known as pelota. 'By God!' says the fatter attendant whose paw
is still comfortably navigating his belly. 'You could get tennis
balls from piles all right!' Soon after this an obese woman from
the lodge inside the gates appears on her doorstep with her right
index finger placed horizontally on her left index finger to sym-
bolize Tea. The attendants at once abandon their patient who
hangs his hands, clasped, between his thighs and contemplates
the earth they have been discussing until a refined Saxon female
voice says, 'Good awfternoon, Mister Cornfield.'

He rises and bows.

'Good afternoon, Miss Huggard.'

The lady and the lunatic sit side by side. Some three miles
farther on, she teaches in a tiny rural Protestant school a few
remnant children of the Reformation. He sees her almost every
day, in fine weather, at this hour, appearing underneath the
tunnel of trees that mark the penultimate stage of her daily
three-mile trudge out to the school and back to the old family
home of the Huggards, a tall weather-slated house that has
stood in its own grounds outside the town for four generations,
and of which she is now the only occupant. She stretches out her
feet and surveys her brogues. He knows what she is about to
say: she says it every time.

'Those skates won't lawst me another month. Every yeah I
weah out three paihs of boots going east and west. So you are
back?' she adds in astonishment and admiration. 'I missed you,
you know. Back from London!' she annotates, as if he were
Marco Polo. 'It was naughty of you, I gathah, to have run
away?'

'The caged bird always flies away,' he laughs.

'And how is good old London?' she asks as breezily as a
games mistress – if games mistresses ever reach fifty.

'Not much different really since I saw it last. Which was
eleven years ago. Too many people. More coloureds. Noisier.
When did you see London last, Miss Huggard?'

'I was there only once, Mister Cornfield. When I was fifteen. Just before the war. Daddy met me at Victoria Station, and took me by Underground down to the docks. The next place I set foot on was the Barbados. As a rule, women, it appears, are not very popular aboard ships, but I had great fun. But of course I was not a woman, I was just Captain Huggard's little girl.'

The word 'Barbados' had visibly excited him.

'Are they wonderful, the Barbados?'

'Rather Britishish. Of course in a long, long ago way. A bit ungainly. I suppose they are all changed now.'

She grimaced and spread her hands in a long, long ago way. Rather ungainly, with her sand-grey hair, her humble spinster's eyes, her stooped back. He wished she did not have to feel that the one adventurous image of her life had altered.

'My father was drowned in 1943. I had just got my teacher's diploma. It was very fortunate. I was free to look after Mummy.'

The walls had closed early on her. She smiled, looked towards the distant outline of her home.

'There was a First World War song called "The Last Long Mile." I've got to face it. Tell me! Does your recent escapade mean that now that you have shown that you can travel you may at last be allowed to visit the town? Walk the roads? You might even visit my school? Wouldn't that be jolly!'

'It may work the other way around. They may now feel confirmed in their notion that I am irresponsible.'

'Oh, dear! I do hope not, Mr Cornfield.'

She rose. He rose.

'I have stolen some begonia bulbs for you,' he said in a naughty-boy voice. 'If you come up to the corner by the land steward's house this evening before the supper bell I'll have them for you.'

'I will come. I do hope you may continue to help the gardener, Mr Cornfield. Your trouble is you do not occupy your mind enough. Work is good for the soul. It is always pleasant talking with you, Mr Cornfield.'

She smiled again, he lifted his cap as she walked away from him. How Protestant!

His two caretakers presently returned and sat on either side of him. Over their tea they had decided that flags underneath their bottoms and flags underneath their feet would be best of all, about which they became so excited that they had barely time to salute Doctor Reynolds in her scarlet sports Triumph, her black curls leaping in the wind as she whirled through the gateway so sharply that her front fender barely missed its left pillar.

Her eyebrows soared with pleasure. He was back! She had a snapshot of him in her side mirror rising to bow after her the way he always used to do. As she sped up the avenue she was still chuckling at his cap lifting sedately from his head inclining baronially, as if he owned the whole blooming madhouse. Odd how those old-fashioned ways of his got on the nerves of every doctor in the place except herself. 'Cornfield's *folie de grandeur*!' – until she gave them their answer one night at dinner.

'So far as I can see the only unusual thing about his manners is that they are so good: the one man in the place who knows how to treat a lady properly.'

They had guffawed of course, but she knew she had drawn a spot of blood: also from herself, who had taken a whole year to pick him out from among the hopeless herds brought in here from the moors, the mountains and the dying islands, mooing as softly and ceaselessly as a village pound. Yet all he had done that morning four years ago had been to waist-bow to a nurse who had responded with a wink and provocative cock of the ankle. A nurse had known how to handle him. She had never known whether to treat him as a patient or as a man.

She braked in the doctors' parking space at the top of the avenue, got out, banged the door and stood glaring across the river valley ridges of Magharamore. She conjured up from behind it the narrow glen of the Owenaheensha. She had fished both rivers many times but there was really no good fishing that way until you came to the lakes of Laoura. She slewed her head eastward to a round hill, ten miles away, horned like Moses by two beams of upthrown sun. Every horizon shouldered white clouds that shouldered more white clouds, that shouldered still more clouds up and up into the deepening blue. Below her the daffodils scattered about the grounds did not sway. The air smelled freshly of the Easter rains. In exasperation she ruffled her poll. She would give it to him straight this time.

'Jack, you damned fool! You've balloxed it for keeps. For years you've been telling us that all you want is to be allowed to stroll around the roads and into the town for an hour a day. Solid John C. Reliable John C. To prove it he runs away from us to London. And then, after six months of A.W.O.L. here he comes crawling back like the Prodigal Son.' She knew that what she would actually say would be, 'Welcome home, Mister Cornfield. I trust you know that you were mad to have left this madhouse. In your five years among us nothing became you less than your leaving us, and nothing more than your return to the village pound.' He would laugh politely. He always saw through her defensive jokes. The one thing she would not dare to say would be, 'I missed you.'

She started to empty her car, furiously throwing the stuff on the cement – rod, waders, basket, suitcase. She became aware of a familiar smell. That would be Mac, pipe smoking, delivered through the revolving glass doors, his lean cheeks insucked, his heavy eyelids lowering at her legs. He would not speak until she deigned to turn. She finally did. He lifted his pipe silently. She noted that he was not coming forward to help her with her gear. If she had been a pretty nurse . . .

'Nice holiday, Doctor Reynolds?' he asked circumspectly.

'Yes, if you don't mind lashing rain, and a force ten gale. If I'd been a flying fish I might have caught a flying fisherman. I played poker, drank Irish, chain smoked and read six whodunits.'

'And won every game hand down I bet? And drank them all under the table? And had the villain spotted by page fifteen?'

'One has to shine at something.'

'You shine! Your boyfriend is back.'

She stared him down.

'So London didn't work?'

'We warned them, didn't we? Six months to the day. I'd have given him six weeks. He stayed with his daughter, that fat, rich American Jewess who kidnapped him from us in October. Four days ago he bombed her. Two black eyes, a crushed rib and a broken septum.'

'Good for him! She is a right bitch.'

'On that, doctor, if on little else we are of one mind. There were occasions when even I felt my toe itching. However, you and I, not being mental patients – so far – can afford to dream violently. With him, an itch today, a black eye tomorrow, a knife the day after.'

She faced him full and crossly, her yellow sou'wester in one fist, her gaff in another.

'I have repeatedly pointed out to you, Doctor MacGowan, that Cornfield is as sane as I am. Even if you think that's not saying very much.'

Furiously she turned her back on him, threw down gaff and sou'wester, rummaged for her bookbag. He would be looking at her bottom now. He spoke pleadingly.

'Judy!'

She turned.

'I missed you.'

'Lookit, Mac. Are you by chance jealous of Cornfield?' He scoffed defensively. 'Then why can't you lay off me? The place is full of passionate nurses mad for it.' She switched herself off. 'How did he get back?'

'His American son-in-law threw him on a plane at London airport last Sunday morning. With a fiver stuffed into his vest pocket. At a quarter to one this Tuesday morning I was awakened by somebody at my doorbell. An old hand, he knows all the ways in. I hauled up the window. There was your ladyship's lordship below on my doorstep shouting against the wind and rain for God's sake to let him in. He was like a water rat with his big, effluent knob of a nose. We had quite an interesting chat, roaring up and down to one another at the tops of our voices. I've never seen such a night. I wouldn't have left a milk bottle out on such a night. No hat. No overcoat. He'd eaten nothing since he left the plane. Hiked the whole way. He was carrying a cardboard suitcase containing dirty linen, a large photograph of his daughter and two small pictures of her that he had been painting. I let him in, poked up the fire, gave him a hot toddy and watched him steam larger than life. That man has a superb constitution. You saw him just now, fresh as a daisy after being storm-battered for nearly forty hours.' One side of his knife-edged mouth smiled. 'While I am deciding what to do with him next I have sent him up to Ward Three.'

Her voice soared.

'Now why the hell should I have the silly bugger under my care?'

He looked paternally at her over his glasses.

'We all have our special babies, Judy. Admit you are pleased to have him back.'

'Not particularly,' she said, sulkily lowering her owl-lidded eyes. 'I have lost interest in his case. He is simply a sound, healthy, ordinary, bad-tempered man whom we have ruined by domesticating, nationalizing, habituating, acclimatizing or, in the neologistic gobbledygook of our bombastic profession, institutionalizing so thoroughly that he is now afraid to live a normal life. We have turned him into that well-established male Irish type, the baa-ram bleating for his mummy's teats. Which we provide. Self-absorbed? Self-pitying? Egocentric? Chip on the shoulder? Truculent? Timid? Incurably self-referential? All that, but even if he really did give his blonde cow of a daughter a couple of shiners does that make him insane? Any more than it would if you were to marry me as you say you would like to, but would not, and gave me two pandas when you discovered the sort of bitch you would sooner or later decide I am? That would not be you walloping me. It would be your dear little ego revenging itself on the whole monstrous regiment of women from Old Mother Hubbard, and Old Mother Goose, and Holy Mum the Church, down to Mother Ireland and your own dear departed and long-suffering Mother Machree. Doctor MacGowan!' She said it sweetly and gently. 'Why have I to explain these elementary things to you so often? Did you never, when younger perhaps, think of taking up plumbing, or dentistry, or some other study a bit more obvious than psychiatry?'

'Some day, Judy,' he said quietly, 'I will black your fucking eye without the blessing of either Father Freud or Mother Church and it might do you a power of good. Meanwhile . . .'

She barely felt the trap snap on her neck.

'. . . I have been rereading your dossier on Cornfield. This afternoon, in fact. You stress that he should be allowed a limited freedom. I think you are on the right track. If this man can travel once to London why should he not travel twice? Turn the matter over again in your mind, Doctor Reynolds. If we are in accord I propose to tell Mrs Reuther that she must henceforth accept full custody and responsibility for her father. In London. Or in New York. Or wherever else she damned well likes.'

He turned to go. The shrillness of her voice halted and turned him.

'Mac! You can't do this! You can't encourage this poor devil to get attached to us – and then boot him out into the streets of London.'

'Isn't it what you have always been asking for on his behalf? Freedom of the city?'

'Not of London! What is he going to do in the purlieus of Sloane Square, Lowndes Street, Kinnerton Street, Eaton Square, Belgravia? A man who has been accustomed for five years to sitting on the side of a country road watching that evening sun go down, chatting with passers-by, looking at a spider in the grass, the drops of dew hung out to dry on a cobweb, able to sit in the gate-lodge by the fireside in the winter with Patrice's fat wife, poke the coals, lift the curtains, look at the flooded river, look . . .'

With a sob, incoherently, she waved around to the grey-stemmed daffodils and the climbing clouds.

His voice became precise and hateful.

'This may be pointed out to his daughter. We have done our bit. See you at dinner,' and the glass valves of the door whirled the blues and whites of the sky behind his back.

'Damn you!' she said bitterly at the slowing doors. Then, luggage-laden, she bumped up the stairs to her rooms.

At the window she took up her old bird-watching binoculars. He was there still, a blurred figure sitting on the low wall, alone. She focused him to sharpness. His back to the fields, his hands hanging between his knees, he was looking at the earth. Suddenly he rose, straightened, braced his aching back, lifted his Atlas arms to grasp the sky. A fine figure of a man, six foot one, red nose like a sailor, brisk black hair. Aged fifty? Not much in his head. Soft-cored. Too gentle. A bit of a coward? She hungered to eat him. She had never seen him stripped but Mac, who had checked his condition several times, reported that he had the physique of a man of thirty. My soul thirsts for him in this wet and rainy land where there is no sun. I want him where every woman longs for the leap of a child. What do I see in him? Myself.

She laid down her field-glasses, drew a hot bath, stripped, and filled herself a glass of Irish. She glanced at her mirrored face, her bulldog nostrils, pocked skin, big mouth, prognathous jaw, laid herself in her hot bath and slowly sipped her liquor. She glanced along her full fish-length in the bath, calmly aware that the gods had never created a more preeminently beautiful body, as far as the neck. She cheerfully informed her wriggling toes, 'If I had been dug up in marble two hundred years ago as a headless Venus I'd be in the Louvre now under spotlights.'

Her eyes wandered out of her bathroom to her bookbag squatting like a black cat in the middle of the carpet of her living-room. *Jessica's Daughter.* According to his publisher, 'John Cornfield's magnificent 100,000 words cry for Freedom.' He should have been dug up as a brainless gladiator. Four months it had taken her to wheedle it out of his besotted daughter, and then only under a solemn promise that nobody else, not even he, must know that a copy of the novel still existed.

Now, it may be agreed that every visible and celestial achievement is, in the nature of nature, flawed. That thing was an embarrassment. Autobiographical as she had expected, which was why she wanted it; and almost straight auto-biography at that, which was why it was a failure. When she was a student at Westminster Hospital she had had a lover who was a real writer who had made her see that the truth is always much too complicated to be told straight out. Here everything was as implacably grim as grime. The hero, like the author, a lone child. Named Shawn. Scene, a grey English mining town. Father and mother Irish-born, Roman Cats, elementary school teachers. At twenty Shawn flies from insensitive and brutal

181

England to warmhearted, kindly Ireland. She snorted. What John-Shawn had fled from was the War, the blackout, roving searchlights, ack-ack, austerity. End of Book One. Dublin. Our hero is found working in Dublin. On an R.C. magazine. That word had always amused her: a storehouse for explosives, the part of a rifle where you put bullets, French for a shop. This shop provokes his last wild cry for freedom when he meets a Jewish girl, named Jessica, visiting Ireland from New York, loses his virginity to her, marries her, gets booted out by his warm-hearted and kindly employers, disowned by his father and mother and angrily returns to cruel, cloddish England. End of Book Two. Fleet Street. Updating obituaries and checking sports results. Lives in a flat in a demi-detached in Crouch End. Constant quarrels with wife. Conscience in flitthers. Drinks. A chaste and tender friendship with an Irish prostitute whose conscience is also in flitthers. And then, casually, simultaneously and without warning he fathers a beautiful daughter and a highly successful novel. Peace? Achievement? Freedom?

In real life *Jessica's Daughter* had been a flop.

To his credit, by the time she was compiling his original dossier, he was able to refer to this fiasco with a bitter humour. But he could not remember even the titles of his four subsequent, unpublished novels.

'Four? What persistence, Mr Cornfield! Still, I hope you enjoyed writing them?'

'I hated every moment of them. Every one of those bloody things,' his cassette recorded, 'was written under the whip of the most characteristically bossy conceited insensitive ambitious misanthropic egomaniacal woman who ever issued out of the loins of Abraham.'

A pity he did not wait another few years before writing these failures. He would have had at least a splendid ending for one of them.

The cassette again:

'We came back to Ireland on holidays eleven years ago she started nagging at me to write a sixth novel one morning I saw red for ten seconds I've often timed it I went for her with a loose brick we had to keep the door of the kitchen open a cottage we hired a small pink Georgian brick six inches by three it didn't do her any harm only for all that blood streaming down her face and she running around in a circle like a dog with the distemper and poor little Beryl staring.'

His wife was probably right to commit him to a private clinic and go back to New York with the kid. Five years later she died, the cash stopped, they had to take him in.

She sucked down the last drops of her whiskey, deposited the glass on the bath mat, sat up and slowly and softly began to soap her armpits and her lavish breasts. Eleven years behind walls and, in her view, only one symptom of abnormality: the pathetic smallness of his protest against his life of a cast-away – his plea to be granted sixty minutes a day alone. Crusoe would probably have got that way in the end, with no more than an occasional dreamy wish to walk on Tower Hill or Cheapside. Still, Crusoe had coped, made a new world. There was nothing wrong with Jack Cornfield except that at some time his wish to cope had got a knockout blow. In what part of him, why, where, nobody would ever know, unless some psychiatrist had him every week for five years, breaking him down and down until he was a little naked man at the bottom of a deep, dark cone begging for the last cruel drop of truth to be squeezed from him – the price of his release to the upper air.

Am I his female Orpheus?

She clambered out of her bath, grumbling 'Cure thyself,' towelled herself with energy, began to dress. She leaned to her mirror to test her upper lip. 'The passing shadow on her upper lip ... Blown hair about her mouth ... Thy shadow, Cynara ... Swan's neck and dark abundant hair ...' She stiffened. Her watch said six thirty. She rang the head nurse of Ward Three. If it was convenient could Mr Cornfield be sent to her surgery at eight o'clock for ten minutes. No, nothing special.

'But we may have to have a conference about him tomorrow morning.'

He was waiting in her office. She lifted down the overcoat hanging on the back of the door.

'I think, Mr Cornfield, we might stroll. It is still bright. I shan't keep you ten minutes.'

They strolled to the highest and quietest corner of the grounds, just below the farm and the land steward, Billy Victory's house. He recognized the clatter from the kitchens after the usual tasteless meal. If he could only have a glass of beer sometimes with his supper. The country slowly expanded. Soon it would be veiled. She talked about her fishing. He asked if it was very far away and she waved towards the horizon. He asked in which direction, and when she pointed he paused and stared. She waited and watched.

They came to the white seat, cast iron, where he had sat an hour ago with Elsie Huggard, giving her six corms of gladioli in a cardboard box marked *Saint Senan's Confectionery*. The name was a common eponym in the town – Saint Senan's Maternity Home, School, Church, Bridge, Furnishing, Insurance, Credit Union, Hospital, Cemetery. The old Huggard home had the Saint's name carved on the pillars of its entrance gate.

'I'm glad to see you back, Mr Cornfield. I hope you realize how mad you were to have left this madhouse.' (Like her to call it that. Honest. No palaver.) 'In all your years nothing became you less than your leaving us and nothing more than your return to the fold.' He laughed obligingly. Who did she think she was fooling? 'Why did you let Mrs Reuther kidnap you away from us?'

He smiled his crooked smile, replied circumspectly:

'Beryl is half-Irish, half-American. And a hundred per cent Jewish. Married to a Jew. Eat your spinach. Drink your chicken soup. One obeys.'

A plane hummed over. Its wingtips blinked. Escaping to London, New York, Amsterdam, or Paris, Brussels?

'I missed you,' she said to the grass.

'I thought of you many times,' he said to the sky, and accepted one of her cigarettes. Her lighter ran a line down the shinbones of her legs. It incised the aquiline face of a revolutionary sucked dry by years of jail. At the sense of so much helplessness in so strong a body a surge of power hit her like a contraction of the womb, a four-beat stoppage of the heart. Her cigarette flew in an arc of anger against the deepening sky. She spoke out of the corner of her mouth like a gangster's moll.

'What are you going to do, Mr Cornfield, when we send you back to your daughter in London?'

'Could you?' he demanded so fiercely that she slewed her head a full hundred and eighty degrees the better to relish his smell of fear, sweat, tobacco.

'If you can travel once you can travel again.' She sweetened her voice. 'You have a very pretty daughter. A lovely girl.'

'Isn't she though?' Eagerly.

'You must be very proud of her.'

'She's all I have in the world.'

'Then why did you go for her, break her nose, crack her ribs, black her pretty eyes?'

He patted her knee. She dribbled for him.

'Me go for Beryl? I just said I did that in order to get back to my featherbed.'

'In that case you should not be here. Perhaps you never even attacked your wife?'

'Now her I did do! With a hammer.'

'You said with a brick, six by three, pink, Georgian.'

'I can't remember. Do you think I'm lying?'

'If you can't remember it's probably true.'

'But little Beryl! For God's sake, not Beryl! It wasn't she pushed me out of that flat in Sloane Square, it was her husband, not that I blame him, he got me four jobs, I couldn't keep any of them, he was quite nice about it, really. One day he even called me "chum." He has his own life to lead, and Beryl is expecting. He had a drink with me at the airport, he stuffed two fivers into my pocket, I drank them in Dublin. I tell you this because you are the only person I can trust in this bin. Will I be chucked out?'

She looked around her. All she could see clearly was a row of lighted windows.

'Mr Cornfield, you did attack your wife with intent to kill. Please let us be clear about that, and no nonsense. You did attack your daughter. And let us have no shilly-shallying about that either. You put them both in mortal danger. You gave your Beryl two shiners, broke her septum, cracked two of her ribs, in a word went off your chump again. Do you understand?'

'I am not,' he said furiously, 'I repeat *not*, off my chump.'

She lifted her eyes imploringly to the one great planet in the sky.

'In that case you wish me to report that you are as gentle as a mouse? That you never really went berserk? That you never will, that you are fit to pack your bag, leave this featherbed and earn your living out there in that dark, wide, windy world? Do you understand all that, you great, big stupid slob?'

He became as gentle as a mouse.

'I am not insane and I will never say otherwise. It simply happens that I do not like this horrible world. And that is your own word. Or, you said it, quoting Bertrand Russell, "This world," you said he said, "is horrible! Horrible! Horrible! Once we admit that we can enjoy the beauty of it." '

'I ought not to have repeated the witticism to somebody only too eager to take my every lightest word seriously. After all, His Lordship might just as well have said, "This world is lovely! Lovely! Lovely! Once we admit that we are ready to suffer the horrors of it." I find plenty of pleasant things sandwiched between the horrors of life. Good fishing. Good drink. Good friends.'

'I do not fish. I do not drink. I have no friends.'

She considered the bizarre angle of his hairy cap against the stars. She wished only that she could strip him, scrub him in a hot, hot bath, and dress him like a free man.

'So be it, Mr Cornfield. You must make your own miserable decisions. And if you still do not like this horrible ship we are sailing in there is a very simple way to solve your tiny problem.'

She drew her index finger across his bristly throat, shivered at the nutmeg-grater feel of it, jumped up and abruptly walked away. 'Damn you!' he shouted after her and sulkily watched her stately figure sink from sight down the hill.

She felt her pulse banging in her right ear. Her calves were groggy. Mac's black house rose against the ash of the Easter moon. Their passionate widower. Twice married. Father of seven. If I became his third they certainly would not become fourteen. She halted to reconnoitre. Doctors were entitled to receive friends in their rooms provided they were not patients or nurses, whether M. or F., but in this fortified village everybody saw, suspected, invented, scoffed, hinted. Even as she looked around she saw a white edge of skirt, a shoe, a stocking, a black cloak slide through young Carty's door. In such matters Mac was neither a Puritan nor a Paul Pry, but if he suspected her of trying to saddle him with Cornfield he would not give her a grass blade of leeway.

There was no corner inside these walls where they could meet after dark. No corner where some eye, some fly, some spy would not sooner or later surprise them. But would either of us dare to? Can a bird fly with a broken wing? A man who had not had a woman for eleven years? That story he told about himself when he was a kid and the fledgling jackdaw that their yard-cat in Stockport struck down with a crooked claw. How he capped it under a cardboard box, and then put this box into a larger box, and then covered that larger box with wire netting, and found a worm for the bird, and gave it a saucer of water, hoping it would recover from the shock, and its wing would mend and it would be able to fly away again.

'But in the morning it was on its side, its eyes glazed, half-closed, its claws and feet extended. Even my worm was dead. The nights in the North can be bitter.'

Well, Judy? And how is our precious cornfed baby? You have become a cat who walks by night. You never drop in for a drink with me these nights. If I may make so bold, Dr Reynolds, am I wrong in imagining that you have, so to speak, been avoiding me lately? Damn you, Jack Cornfield, you know the form just as well as I do. No, Mac! For the hundredth time. No! And if I did let you that night after Easter it was not, I assure you, because I was madly in love with you but simply that I felt randy as hell and sorry for all poor, bloody mankind. Oh, yes indeed, Dr MacGowan, I cannot tell you how happy I am here, safe from all temptations and troubles, all of us together in this cosy little world of our own. Oh, you just reminded me, Mr Cornfield, I have a book about the South Pacific that you might like to collect from my office this evening . . .

A week later she applied for a post in Dublin. On the night she told him so eleven years of celibacy fell from his back. Hand in hand, like children, they ran for their lives. Three weeks later they were married. To establish his pride his Beryl settled a generous income on him. Elsie Huggard said to him, 'While you are looking for a house why don't you rent my ground floor? "Saint Senan's" is big enough the Lord knows, built to house ten children at least. I shan't butt in on you.' He accepted without even examining the house, but when the two of them first entered it he was as boastful and triumphant as if he had inspected it as carefully as a real estate broker.

'I couldn't have chosen better. See! A ship's bell, with the name engraved on it. PYLADES. A Turkish hookah. A sailing ship inside a Barbados rum bottle. An Indian coffee table, brass inlaid. A Moroccan tapestry. Junk from all over the globe. I bet you we'll come on a fifty-year-old album of photographs. The place smells of the seven seas.'

She laughed at his zany laughter, told him he was like a lark in the air, whereupon, without embarrassment, he recited, and at the end slid into song: *'Dear thoughts are in my mind / And my soul soars enchanted / When I hear the dear lark sing / In the clear air of the day. / For a tender, beaming smile / To my hopes has been granted / And I know my love tonight will come / And will not say me nay.'*

'You entertain strong feelings, Mr Cornfield.'

'And what other feelings would you expect your husband to entertain for his wife, Dr Reynolds?'

Every day he wandered the streets of the town, or along the tunnelled, bug-bright roads of Spring. Every evening, over dinner, her first question was always, 'What sage did you meet today? What wisdom did you collect?' and he would empty a pocketful into her lap, a word, a leaf, a stone, a broken eggshell, a sound, a chestnut, a colour, an acorn, a feather. For a long time she puzzled over the inordinate amount of satisfaction he could get out of the slightest bit of chat on a road, in a field, a side street. She decided in the end that he was extending, expanding, marrying everybody and everything, giving birth by communion with other selves. For eleven years he had been imprisoned on a barren island. At last, she smiled proudly, her odd man out, coupling like an unspancelled goat.

She watched him intently. She knew her man better than he her. She observed that his strolls changed from walks to expeditions, extending farther and farther. He bought a bicycle to go farther still. She noted that he would not come salmon fishing with her, hating, so he said, that prolonged playing of the hooked fish in from the wide ocean; but she noticed that when she took down her trout rod he came, she teased, illogically, although he insisted that he came then only because he liked the long drive across the parallel ridges of Magharamore, and the Owenaheensha on to Lough Laoura. She noted further that on their return he would always ask her to pull up on some ridge where he would alight and look back.

One day he asked the question outright. 'What's out there behind those Laoura mountains?' and was patently astonished when she just said, 'Another county. No fishing. Shallow streams.'

The testing time came with the winter, cold, wet and seemingly endless. Work and fishing sufficed to distract her. He felt bottled up. The town offered few distractions. She suggested a trip to London but the look he gave her silenced her. The wintry roads discouraged him although he was abashed every morning to see Elsie Huggard start off on her three-mile trudge, head bowed into the weather, cowled under a shining black mackintosh down to her ankles. He watched television all day, or sat reading by the fire, mostly historical biographies, histories of exploration, travel books. He developed a taste for astronomy, had a brief craze for books on mountaineering. She hated to think of him sitting there in silence, his book sinking to his lap, his eyes facing an unseen fire, and for the first time a truth about him that she had always known in an abstract way became visually real – he had been beaten into subjectivity by years of loneliness. They had not killed his spirit, but he would always be at risk.

Driving home one dank, dusky, February afternoon, the hood of her red Triumph closed tight, she was startled to see him standing beside the gate-lodge greeting her with his old polite bow and raised hat. He sat in beside her; for one second, perhaps for as long as two, he smiled at her dilated eyes and then burst into a laugh.

'It's all right, darling. I am not suffering what is known as a regression to a chronologically earlier pattern of feeling. I just came up to have a chat with old Dawson the cook.'

'About what?' Suspiciously.

'He used to be a ship's cook. He sailed the seven seas in his heyday. I've been reading a book about Gauguin in Tahiti. Are you going fishing this weekend?'

'Come?'

'Yes. I could leave you at the lake and drive on. I want to see what's beyond those Laoura hills.'

'But you don't drive!'

'I've been taking lessons secretly,' he said with his naughty-boy grin. 'I got my licence yesterday.'

She said nothing for a long minute. Then she said that that was a fine idea. All the same he really might have mentioned it to her? He asked her if she would not, in that case, have wanted to teach him herself; at which she admitted that it is, apparently, all too easy for a wife to begin behaving like a wife.

He duly drove her to her chosen corner of the lake, promised to meet her in the afternoon at the local pub, drove away. Twilight came. He did not. She had a drink while waiting. He did not come. She had another drink. She kept glancing at her watch. Her hands were tight. He came. When he did not say he was sorry for being late she found it hard not to behave like a wife; wondered was he finding it hard to behave like a husband. He asked her easily as they drove away how she had fared.

'Nothing worth talking about. A couple of brown trout. Under a pound each. You?'

'In the distance between two clefts of hills like breasts I saw a V of sea.'

'That,' she said sourly, 'means you were only ten thousand miles away from Tahiti.'

He comforted her knee.

'When Gauguin was a child he went to Peru, came home, sailed with the merchant marine and the French navy, chucked

it, got a job, married, chucked it when he was thirty-six, tried
Brittany, sailed for Martinique, chucked it, tried Paris again,
chucked it, tried Brittany again, sailed to Tahiti, lived and
painted there, chucked it, sailed for the Marquesas, and died.
Let's fry our brown trout.'

For some fifteen miles the windscreen wipers hissed. Then the
mist stopped, the sky cleared, and for the rest of the drive they
were aware of a vast tumescence of moon in command of all
wintry life. Immediately they got into their dusty old living-
room in 'Saint Senan's' he lit the laid fire. When it was blazing
they sat before it with two whiskeys, exchanging trifles about
their day. Presently he got up and went into the kitchen – old,
flagged, vast, that nobody had refurbished for forty years. He
came back wearing her butcher's blue-and-white apron, and
went to her fishing basket for the two fish. She got up to help,
but he waved her back commandingly.

'You stay there. I'm going to gut 'em and cook 'em.
Meunière? Fresh butter just turning brown. A touch of
lemon? A spot of parsley? Plates straight from oven to table.'
He winked at her over his disappearing shoulder. 'This I *can*
do.'

'But I'd like to help!'

'I need no help,' he said arrogantly and left her.

She sank back into her armchair and, without relish, finished
her drink. Presently she heard him humming over his chopping
block. To command her feelings she inhaled slowly and slowly
exhaled, aware that something far less than a chorus ending
from Euripides or a sunset touch would be more than enough to
make her burst into tears at her Grand Perhaps singing over her
two fish. Suddenly he reappeared in the door of the kitchen with
a look of farcical helplessness, advanced, turned his shoulders
to her and asked her to tighten those damned strings, so she
knotted the cords more tightly and with an approving pat on the
bottom sent him on his way.

When he was gone she covered her face with her palms and
began blowing into them like waves dying in caves. This was, no
doubt, since it had so happened, and, after all, Saint Augustine
once said that whatever is is right, exactly what was to be ex-

pected, but it was not at all what she had wanted. She blew one last mighty wave of discontent into her hands, rose and listened to him tra-la-la-laing merrily through the Blue Danube waltz. Then, with a philosophic smile she dutifully began to lay the table. For what, as Aeschylus says, can be more pleasing than the ties of host and guest? To drown his tra-la-la-laing she murmured to herself certain famous lines by another prisoner that had always entertained her:

> If I have freedom in my love,
>   And in my soul am free,
> Angels alone that soar above
>   Enjoy such libertee.